Contents

Dear Puzzler,

Why try your hand, or more importantly your brain, at solving the puzzles in this edition of Mind Stretchers?

The puzzles have been designed to stimulate the many different cognitive skills we need to successfully handle the world around us. Some of these skills decline with age or from lack of use but they can be improved by exercising the very circuits targeted by our puzzles. In this way, solving a puzzle begins the cure! You may find that your mood also improves when you work on puzzles and get them right, thanks to your brain's own reward system releasing the neurotransmitter serotonin.

To this end, there are plenty of problems to be tackled in this edition of Mind Stretchers, from complex to simple. Math is a useful tool which can be applied to many real-world situations. If you are a "words" person who would prefer to skip the number puzzles—please don't. The ability to strip a problem of its emotional content and quantify its values involves sophisticated mental gymnastics. Similarly, to tease out the logic of a sentence is a complex skill involving semantic knowledge, concentration and judgment arising from previous experience.

At the other end of the spectrum, something as simple as a word search has real value as a test of concentration and word recognition, while the puzzles at the foot of the pages provide many opportunities for vocabulary building.

For the fun of it, you might want to set a timer or let someone else try the same puzzle and compare scores. So grab a pencil and have a good time, as it were, with these cognitive calisthenics!

Allen D. Bragdon
Mind Stretchers Puzzle Editor

CROSSWORDS WORD SEARCHES
LOGIC PUZZLES & SURPRISES!

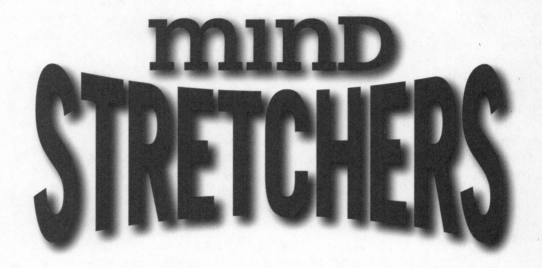

mind STRETCHERS

SANGRIA EDITION

EDITED BY ALLEN D. BRAGDON

Reader's Digest

The Reader's Digest Association, Inc.
New York / Montreal

Project Staff

PROJECT EDITOR
Robert Ronald

PUZZLE EDITOR
Allen D. Bragdon

PRINCIPAL PUZZLE AUTHORS
Peter De Schepper
Frank Coussement
John M. Samson
Sam Bellotto Jr.

CONTRIBUTING PUZZLE AUTHOR
Ron Grosset

SERIES ART DIRECTOR
Andrée Payette

DESIGNER
Craig Brown

PRODUCTION ARTIST
Chris A. Cant

ILLUSTRATIONS
BrainSnack®

COPY EDITOR
Judy Yelon

PROOFREADER
Penny Grearson

MANAGER, ENGLISH BOOK EDITORIAL
Pamela Johnson

VICE PRESIDENT, BOOK EDITORIAL
Robert Goyette

The Reader's Digest Association, Inc.

PRESIDENT AND CHIEF EXECUTIVE OFFICER
Robert Guth

EXECUTIVE VICE PRESIDENT, RDA & PRESIDENT, NORTH AMERICA
Dan Lagani

EXECUTIVE VICE PRESIDENT, RDA & PRESIDENT, EUROPE
Dawn Zier

CHIEF CONTENT OFFICER
Liz Vaccariello

ISBN 978-1-55475-105-1

Address any comments about *Mind Stretchers, Sangria Edition* to:

Reader's Digest Association (Canada) ULC
Book Series Editor
1100 Rene-Levesque Blvd. West
Montreal, Quebec H3B 5H5
Canada

To order copies of this or other editions of the *Mind Stretchers* book series,
call 1-800-846-2100 in the United States and 1-800-465-0780 in Canada.

Visit us on the Web, in the United States at **rd.com**
and in Canada at **readersdigest.ca**

Printed in the United States of America

■ Meet the Authors

Allen D. Bragdon

Allen describes himself as "the whimsical old dog with puzzle experience and a curious mind." He is a member of the Society for Neuroscience, founding editor of *Games* magazine and editor of the Playspace daily puzzle column, formerly syndicated internationally by *The New York Times*. The author of dozens of books of professional and academic examinations and how-to instructions in practical skills, Allen is also the director of the Brainwaves Center.

PeterFrank

PeterFrank was founded in 2000. It is a partnership between High Performance bvba, owned by Peter De Schepper, and Frank Coussement bvba, owned by Frank Coussement. Together they form a dynamic, full-service content provider specialized in media content.They have more than twenty years of experience in publishing management, art/design and software development for newspapers, consumer magazines, special interest publications and new media.

John M. Samson

John M. Samson is currently editor of Simon & Schuster's *Mega Crossword Series*. His crosswords have appeared on cereal boxes, rock album covers, quilts, jigsaw puzzles, posters, advertisements, newspapers, magazines ... and sides of buildings. John also enjoys painting and writing for the stage and screen.

Sam Bellotto Jr.

Sam Bellotto Jr. has been making puzzles professionally since 1979, when he broke into the business by placing his first sale with *The New York Times Magazine* under then crossword puzzle editor Eugene T. Maleska. Sam has been a regular contributor to Simon & Schuster, *The New York Times*, Random House, and magazines such as *Back Stage*, *Central New York*, *Public Citizen* and *Music Alive!* Bellotto's Rochester, NY-based company, Crossdown, develops word-puzzle computer games and crossword construction software.

When Sam is not puzzling he's out hiking with Petra, his black Labrador dog.

BrainSnack®

The internationally registered trademark BrainSnack® stands for challenging, language-independent, logical puzzles and mind games for kids, young adults and adults. The brand stands for high-quality puzzles. Whether they are made by hand, such as visual puzzles, or generated by a computer, such as sudoku, all puzzles are tested by the target group they are made for before they are made available. In order to guarantee that computer-generated puzzles can actually be solved by humans, BrainSnack® makes programs that only use human logic algorithms.

■ Meet the Puzzles

Mind Stretchers is filled with a delightful mix of classic and new puzzle types. To help you get started, here are instructions for each, with tips and examples included.

WORD GAMES

Crossword Puzzles

Clues. Clues. Clues.

Clues are the deciding factor that determines crossword-solving difficulty. Many solvers mistakenly think strange and unusual words are what make a puzzle challenging. In reality, crossword constructors generally try to avoid grid esoterica, opting for familiar words and expressions.

For example, here are some actual clues you'll be encountering and their respective difficulty levels:

LEVEL 1	*Barney Miller* cop
LEVEL 2	Romanov ruler
LEVEL 3	Cambodian currency
LEVEL 4	Rescuer of Odysseus
LEVEL 5	Having big feet

Clues to amuse. Clues to educate. Clues to challenge your mind.

All the clues are there—what's needed now is your answers.

Happy solving!

Word Searches
by PeterFrank

Both kids and grown-ups love 'em, making word searches one of the most popular types of puzzle. In a word search, the challenge is to find hidden words within a grid of letters. In the typical puzzle, words can be found in vertical columns, horizontal rows or along diagonals, with the letters of the words running either forward or backward. You'll be given a list of words to find. But it does not stop there. There is a hidden message—related to the theme of the word search—in the letters left behind after all of the clues have been found. String together those extra letters, and the message will reveal itself.

Hints: *One of the most reliable and efficient searching methods is to scan each row from top to bottom for the first letter of the word. So if you are looking for "violin," you would look for the letter "v." When you find one, look at all the letters that surround it for the second letter of the word (in this case, "i"). Each time you find a correct two-letter combination (in this case, "vi"), you can then scan either for the correct three-letter combination ("vio") or the whole word.*

Word Sudoku
by PeterFrank

Sudoku puzzles have become hugely popular, and our word sudoku puzzles bring a much-loved challenge to word puzzlers.

The basic sudoku puzzle is a 9 x 9 square grid, split into 9 square regions, each containing 9 cells. You need to complete the grid so that each row, each column and each 3 x 3 frame contains the nine letters from the black box above the grid.

There is always a hidden nine-letter word in the diagonal from top left to bottom right.

EXAMPLE

SOLUTION

NUMBER GAMES

Sudoku

by PeterFrank

The original sudoku number format is amazingly popular the world over due to its simplicity and challenge.

The basic sudoku puzzle is a 9 x 9 square grid, split into 9 square regions, each containing 9 cells. Complete the grid so that each row, each column and each 3 x 3 frame contains every number from 1 to 9.

EXAMPLE

SOLUTION

As well as classic sudoku puzzles, you'll also find sudoku X puzzles, where the main diagonals must also include every number from 1 to 9, and sudoku twins with two overlapping grids.

Kakuro

by PeterFrank

These puzzles are like crosswords with numbers. There are clues across and down, but the clues are numbers. The solution is a sum which adds up to the clue number.

Each number in a black area is the sum of the numbers that you have to enter in the empty boxes beside or below. The empty boxes that make up the sum are called a run. The sum of the across run is written above the diagonal in the black area, while the sum of the down run is written below the diagonal.

Runs can contain only the numbers 1 through 9, and each number in a run can only be used once. The gray boxes contain only odd numbers and the white contain only even numbers.

EXAMPLE 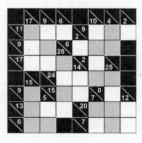 SOLUTION

LOGIC PUZZLES

Binairo

by PeterFrank

Binairo puzzles look similar to sudoku puzzles. They are just as simple and challenging but that is where the similarity ends.

There are two versions: odd and even. The even puzzles feature a 12 x 12 grid. You need to complete the grid with zeros and ones, until there are 6 zeros and 6 ones in every row and every column. No more than two of the same number can be next to or under each other. Rows or columns with exactly the same combination are not allowed.

EXAMPLE	SOLUTION

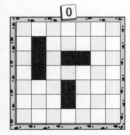

The odd puzzles feature an 11 x 11 grid. You need to complete the grid with zeros and ones until there are 5 zeros and 6 ones in every row and column.

Keep Going

In this puzzle, start on a blank square of your choice and connect as many blank squares as possible with one single continuous line.

You can only connect squares along vertical and horizontal lines, not along diagonals. You must continue the connecting line up until the next obstacle—i.e., the rim of the box, a black square or a square that has already been used.

You can change direction at any obstacle you meet. Each square can only be used once. The number of blank squares left unused is marked in the upper square. There is more than one solution, but we only include one solution in our answer key.

EXAMPLE	SOLUTION

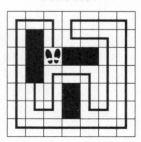

Number Cluster

by PeterFrank

Number Cluster puzzles are language-free, logical numerical problems. They consist of cubes on a 6 x 6 grid. Numbers have been placed in some of the cubes, while the rest are empty. Your challenge is to complete the grid by creating runs of the same number and length as the number supplied. So where a cube with the number 5 has been included on the grid, you need to create a run of five number 5s, including the cube already shown. The run can be horizontal, vertical, or both horizontal and vertical.

EXAMPLE	SOLUTION

Word Pyramid

Each word in the pyramid has the letters of the word above it, plus a new letter.

Start with the answer to clue No.1 and work your way to the base of the pyramid to complete the word pyramid.

Sport Maze

This puzzle is presented on a 6 x 6 grid. Your starting point is indicated by a red cell with a ball and a number. Your objective is to draw the shortest route from the ball to the goal, the only square without a number. You can only move along vertical and horizontal lines, not along diagonals. The figure on each square indicates the number of squares the ball must be moved in the same direction. You can change direction at each stop.

EXAMPLE   SOLUTION

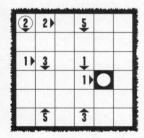

Cage the Animals

This puzzle presents you with a zoo divided into a 16 x 16 grid. The different animals on the grid need to be separated. Draw lines that will completely divide up the grid into smaller squares, with exactly one animal per square. The squares should not overlap.

EXAMPLE   SOLUTION

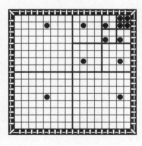

VISUAL PUZZLES

Throughout *Mind Stretchers* you will find unique mazes, visual conundrums and other colorful challenges. Each comes with a new name and unique instructions. Our best advice? Patience and perseverance. Your eyes will need time to unravel the visual secrets.

BrainSnack® Puzzles

To solve a BrainSnack® puzzle, you must think logically. You'll need to use one or several strategies to detect direction, differences and/or similarities, associations, calculations, order, spatial insight, colors, quantities and distances. A BrainSnack® ensures that all the brain's capacities are fully engaged. These are brain sports at their best!

Sunny Weather

We all want to know the weather forecast, and here's your chance to figure it out! Arrows are scattered on a grid. Each arrow points toward a space where a sun symbol should be, but the symbols cannot be next to each other vertically, horizontally or diagonally. A symbol cannot be placed on top of an arrow. You must determine where the symbols should be placed.

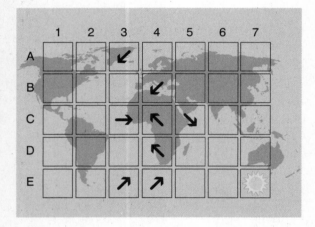

You'll also find more than 100 short brainteasers scattered throughout these pages. These puzzles, found at the bottom of the page, will give you a little light relief from the more intense puzzles while still challenging you.

• ONE LETTER LESS OR MORE

A G E N C I E S -E ☐ ☐ A ☐ ☐ ☐ ☐

• LETTERBLOCKS

W R H * L A O
C A G L L H A

• BLOCK ANAGRAM

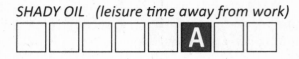

SHADY OIL (leisure time away from work)

☐ ☐ ☐ ☐ ☐ **A** ☐ ☐

• DOODLE PUZZLE

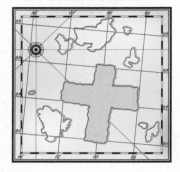

But wait—there's more!

There are additional brainteasers at the top of odd numbered pages, organized into two categories:

• **QUICK!:** These tests challenge your ability to instantly calculate numbers or recall well-known facts.

• **DO YOU KNOW...?:** These more demanding questions probe the depth of your knowledge of facts and trivia.

■ Master Class:

Sleep on It

If you've been racking your brains over a problem all day and without success, your next best bet may be to go to bed and sleep on it. Recent scientific studies show that sleep has the remarkable ability to process a problem and provide insight into the solution.

The dictionary defines "insight" as an instance of apprehending the true nature of a thing through intuitive understanding. There are numerous accounts of scientists developing intuitive understanding, discovering formulas, or arriving at effective conclusions following a good night's sleep. In fact, Mendeleyev was not able to finish construction of the periodic table of elements until a dream gave him insight into the underlying rules behind the symbols.

Sleeping on the job

Exactly how sleep "works" is not clear, but the sleeping brain appears capable of reorganizing and reinforcing memories and new experiences, thus leading to enhanced memory and learning. Just as REM sleep occurs each night without us always being able to remember our dreams, so learning and memory reorganization can happen during sleep without our being aware of it.

In studies on rats, it was found that REM sleep increased after they had learned new tasks, and, if REM sleep was prevented, this learning was impaired. Other studies revealed that when rats were navigating new mazes, neurons fired in specialized brain circuits. Later, when these rats were asleep, the same circuitry became active again.

Similar things occur in the human brain. When an awake-learning experience is strong, it may invade our sleep. It is not uncommon for someone who has spent the day ice skating or skiing to report feeling the illusion of movement at the onset of sleep. People learning a new video game, such as Tetris, often report seeing an intrusive image of the game when dropping off to sleep. Hence, although the body is sleeping, the brain remains active, replaying and reprocessing events experienced while we are awake.

Counting on more than sheep

Scientists have been able to specifically test the affect of sleep on insight into solving problems by giving subjects a specially designed number sequence test—a modified Number Reduction Task.

Subjects were asked to look at a series of eight digits and transform the digits into a new set by applying two simple rules sequentially, from one digit to the next. Discovering another hidden abstract rule, which was not mentioned, would also speed up the answer process considerably. Subjects were trained on three blocks of the task, and then some were asked to go to sleep, and others to stay awake, for eight hours, and come back to be retested on ten blocks of the task.

Retest results showed that those subjects who had slept were more than twice as likely to gain insight into the answer (60% solved it) than those who had remained awake (only 22% solved it). If the subjects were not exposed to the problem before going to sleep they showed no improvement in answering the remaining tasks: thus, sleep could enhance learning only if a subject had been exposed to the test and a memory of it had been formed before going to sleep.

Another interesting fact was noted after analyzing the data from the test results: sleep accelerated the reaction time of non-solvers, but it did not affect the reaction time of the solvers. The slower reaction time of the solvers is thought to be due to the time it takes for the brain to overlap memory representation of the numbers made during sleep with those occurring during conscious memory and task performance. Hence, while sleep may provide insight, it does not necessarily come in a flash; indeed, it may take a while for the brain to combine unconscious associations made during sleep with those of the wakened world.

Get your zzzz's

While declarative memory (refers to memories which can be consciously recalled such as facts and knowledge) is formed during conscious awareness and depends on a strong hippocampus, apparently, not all learning is conscious. Our daytime experiences are temporarily stored in the hippocampus and later transferred and processed in other parts of the brain during sleep (such as the medial temporal lobes and prefrontal cortical areas). Thus, when we awake in the morning, we may literally be able to see a problem in a "new light." However, it may take several days to a week for the brain to process memories and new information into new solutions, so don't expect all insights to occur in one night.

Also, researchers are still not certain which stage of sleep reworks the memories. There is evidence that explicit memory tasks are sensitive to deprivation of slow-wave sleep, yet many scientific and creative insights have been formed during dreams, which is REM sleep. This indicates that both REM and non-REM sleep are needed for forming optimal memory and learning.

Therefore, getting an undisturbed and complete night's sleep, through all the stages of sleep, is your best strategy for boosting your problem-solving ability. It looks like Mother was right again. There's truth in the adage, "Early to bed, early to rise, makes a man healthy, wealthy and wise."

Testing Memory Skills

TEST 1. Recognition Is Easier Than Cold Recall
Read quickly through the descriptions of famous people below. Limit yourself to about a minute. How many can you name?
•   Hollywood director who played Opie on television's *Andy Griffith Show* and Richie Cunningham in *Happy Days*.
•   Actor who played Perry Mason on the TV show by the same name.
•   Jewish girl who wrote a diary while hiding in an attic in Amsterdam.

- Woman who studies chimpanzees in Africa.
- First American woman in space.
- Greek goddess of wisdom who sprang from the head of Zeus.
- Actress who starred in *A Few Good Men* and *Striptease*.
- Three-time Best Director Academy Award winner for *It's a Wonderful Life* and two other films.
- Founder and spokesman of Wendy's hamburger chain.
- Actress who played opposite Humphrey Bogart in *To Have and Have Not*, and married him a year later.
- Grande Dame of American cooking who starred in TV's *The French Chef*.
- 1995 Best Actress Academy Award winner for her role as Sister Helen Prejean in *Dead Man Walking*.
- Watergate figure who now has his own radio show.
- Founder of CNN, owner of the Atlanta Braves, and Jane Fonda's ex.
- Hatchet-wielding anti-alcohol crusader, circa 1900.

Now look at the end of this Master Class and try again by matching the list of names you see there to the list of questions.

TEST 2. How Well You Remember Depends On What You Already Know

All things being equal, the more you know, the easier it is to remember new things that you can integrate into your pre-existing knowledge base. So, for example, if a researcher were to compare an 80-year-old gardener's memory for the details of the passage that follows with that of a 20-year-old non-gardener, the 80-year-old would likely perform better.

"My mother always enjoyed gardening. For her, winter was a time of deep depression. Each spring, her spirits would rise as she replenished the soil with compost and added new plants to the flower bed. White alyssum and blue lobelia would go on the front border, marking the edge of the bed with a Lilliputian hedgelet of vividly-colored bursts of cloud and azure. Behind the border, she would add plants of medium height, such as dahlias, ranunculus, and snapdragons, which looked to my child's eye, gazing on the garden those spring mornings through my bedroom window, like so much joyous multi-colored birthday confetti. When digging this center strip of the flower bed, she would always take care not to disturb the tulip and daffodil bulbs she had planted the previous autumn, and which were just beginning to poke their pale green noses up from the thawing ground. Rising like giants behind them were the tallest plants forming an almost-solid backdrop against the stucco wall between our yard and the neighbor's. Foxglove, bearded iris and hollyhock loomed there, stately and vain, so gaudily bizarre in their finery that one almost felt them to be foreign interlopers from the Orient or perhaps from Mars."

Now, without looking back, try to answer these questions:
1. List one flower from the front border of the bed, one from the medium height center strip, and one tall one from the rear—in that order.
2. Was the lobelia red?
3. According to the passage, would you expect tulips to be very low, medium, or tall?
4. If the narrator's mother had wanted to plant statice, a plant of medium height, which other plant would she probably have put it next to: lobelia, iris or ranunculus?

5. Of these three, which did the narrator seem to think was the gaudiest: foxglove, ranunculus, snapdragon?

Answers are at the end of the Master Class.

TEST 3. Working Memory Skills Decline With Age

Here's a task designed to test two components of working memory: online processing and short-term memory storage. Ideally, have someone read these sentences aloud to you, slowly and clearly. For each sentence, judge whether it makes sense or not. Some do, some don't. At the same time, remember the word at the end of each sentence that serves as a short-hand summary of the sentence's theme.

1. Novels are accounts of someone's reality, even if that reality exists in nothing but a world of fantasy. STORY

2. A landlord is like the dictator of a land of his own making: he tells his mothers what to do, and they have no choice but to obey. RENT

3. When I was young, I would watch my aunt each November planting bulbs in her pockets. GARDEN

4. College is supposed to be a place where you learn few skills, except the skill of knowing how to learn. STUDY

5. Most young people these days have never learned the value of the kind of sacrifice our softballs had to make. DUTY

6. A trip to the outback can be fun, as long as you stay out of the sun, don't drink too much beer, and avoid getting kicked by a kangaroo. AUSTRALIA

7. The trouble with magnums is that they're too big for one, but not big enough for two. WINE

8. Churchill's wife had a nickname for him that many a biographer has whittled. BULLDOG

Forgotten any of the words yet? To do well on this test, you have to coordinate two cognitive skills: analyzing the meaning of each sentence for semantic incongruities and maintaining a memory of an increasingly long list of words. Older people tend to score lower than younger people on this kind of test.

ANSWERS
Test 1. Recognition Is Easier Than Cold Recall

Answers are in random order, for you to match them up to the descriptions of famous people pages 12–13): Lauren Bacall, Sally Ride, Dave Thomas, Julia Child, G. Gordon Liddy, Anne Frank, Susan Sarandon, Raymond Burr, Carrie Nation, Ron Howard, Jane Goodall, Demi Moore, Frank Capra, Ted Turner, Athena.

At all ages, the first task is harder than the second, since recall requires more effort on the part of frontal-lobe-based retrieval skills than simple recognition. As people age, their frontal lobes participate less and less automatically in recall, so more conscious effort has to be made, but recognition skills remain about the same. For people with dementia, both recall and recognition become difficult.

Test 2. How Well You Remember …

"My mother always enjoyed gardening …"

1. Front: alyssum or lobelia. Center: snapdragon, ranunculus or dahlia (tulip or daffodil OK too). Rear: foxglove, hollyhock or bearded iris

2. It was blue, not red

3. Medium

4. Ranunculus

5. Foxglove

Key:

0–1 correct answers: remind me not to let you take care of my plants while I'm on vacation!

2–3 correct: you seem to know the difference between a wisteria and a weed!

4–5 correct: either you're a gardener, or you have a mind like a steel trap!

★ First-Name Basis by Michele Sayer

ACROSS

1 Thatching palm
5 Sensuous dance
10 Neighbor on
14 Jewish month
15 Inspiration for *Troilus and Cressida*
16 Singer in *Footloose*
17 Sloppily
19 Way up a ski slope
20 Cassava products
21 Place to start a ride
23 Meshuga
24 High interest
25 Army brass
28 Permit access
29 Bawl
32 Jackets and collars
33 Norse love goddess
34 Sugar suffix
35 "What's Hecuba to him ___ to Hecuba": Shak.
36 What Santa holds
37 Religious painting
38 Carry the day
39 Positioned
40 Lower-leg joint
41 ___ Bernardino
42 Stone for a Libra
43 Winter apple
44 Toys on strings
46 Cute and sassy
47 Rink drinks
49 Puts out leaves
53 Arizona neighbor
54 Towel fabric
56 Schwinn product
57 Sister of Terpsichore
58 Conga feature
59 Got an A
60 ___ Hall U.
61 Challenge to a duel

DOWN

1 Statesman Gingrich
2 Hip bones
3 Tooth part
4 Multipurpose
5 Colors lightly
6 Fake handle
7 Rock guitarist Lofgren
8 "Hello! ma ragtime ___ ..."
9 Extended voyages
10 Westminster Abbey feature
11 Anklets
12 Orenburg's river
13 Spare item
18 "___ for the asking"
22 Salad fish
24 Capsize
25 Alley sounds
26 Pompeii courts
27 Corn bread
28 Projecting window
30 "___ Mio"
31 John Brown's eulogist
33 Greek cheeses
36 Snappy comebacks
37 Loads software
39 High-protein bean
40 Goldfinger
43 Swear by
45 Exclaimed surprise
46 ___ Novo (Benin capital)
47 Where the conga was born
48 Of the ear
49 Pledge's group
50 Elbow grease
51 Volcano in Sicily
52 Smith of FOX
55 Before, for a bard

★★ Number Cluster

Complete the grid by constituting adjoining clusters that consist of as many cubes as the number on the cubes. At cube 5, for instance, you will have to make a five-cube cluster. Two or more figure cubes of the same value belong to the same cluster. You can only place your cubes along horizontal and/or vertical lines.

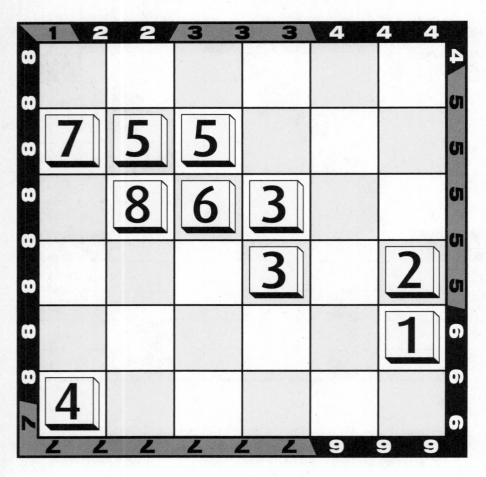

CONNECT TWO

An oxymoron is a combination of seemingly contradictory or incongruous words, such as "science fiction"(science means "knowledge or study dealing with facts or truth" while fiction means "an imagined or invented creation"). Connect the words with meanings that oppose each other and make oxymorons.

BONELESS	SHORTS
ALL	ESTIMATE
LONG	ALONE
FIRM	RIBS

★★ BrainSnack®—Tennis Letters

Which letter should replace the question mark?

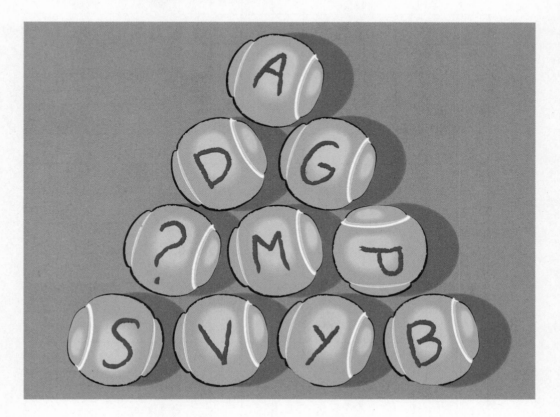

DOUBLETALK

Homophones are words that share the same pronunciation, no matter how they are spelled. If they are spelled differently then they are called heterographs. Find heterographs meaning:

AN INSECT and A RELATION

★ Gigi by Cindy Wheeler

ACROSS

1 Karate blow
5 Far from fresh
10 Give the once-over
14 Drumset company
15 Harness horse
16 Pitt in *Fight Club*
17 Lined up
18 Skylit lobbies
19 Paris bean
20 Comment from "Peanuts"
22 Eucharist holder
23 Canon camera
24 Highlight at the Met
25 Six ___ of separation
29 Included within
32 Lotion lilies
33 French bread
35 Relished a roast
36 Like jokers, at times
37 Follow too closely
38 Gratuitous
39 Auction action
40 Vermont ski resort
41 Polio vaccine pioneer
42 Western hat
44 Moldova and Malawi, e.g.
46 Naldi of silent movies
47 Jazz cornetist Adderley
48 Knights-to-be
50 Weimaraner's nickname
56 Suffix for cell
57 Bingo relative
58 Hightail it
59 Interior designer Berkus
60 Gibson ingredient
61 Forelimb bone
62 Even-steven
63 Just know
64 Boys

DOWN

1 Rock-climbing site
2 Deli sandwich
3 Melville novel
4 Kind of sugar
5 Widely scattered
6 *Mon Oncle* director
7 4,840 square yards
8 Mariner Ericson
9 C.C. Sabathia stat
10 Lay one's hands on
11 1931 star of *Mata Hari*
12 Held up in traffic, say
13 Nice place to live
21 "And so it ___"
22 LPGA members
24 Uncontrollable
25 Sopranos Kotoski and Upshaw
26 *The Mill on the Floss* author
27 Bridge in *A View to a Kill*
28 First U.S.-born saint
29 *The Green Hat* author
30 Oktoberfest mug
31 Adolescents
34 Motor City union
37 Plato's promenade
38 True to one's word
40 Speedy jets of yore
41 Doe's other half
43 Like parking garages
45 "Do I have a volunteer?"
48 Fourth-and-long call
49 Asian range
50 "Singing Cowboy" Autry
51 Drought easer
52 Eve's grandson
53 Pueblo pot
54 E-mail button
55 Sorority receptions
57 Yak genus

★ Sauces

All the words are hidden vertically, horizontally or diagonally—in both directions. The letters that remain unused form a sentence from left to right.

```
D X G N A D A P S A S A U C T
A U O E I S A U S U B S T A A
P O N T C E M T H A T I B S P
U R S R S M A Y O N N A I S E
R A E A U E D R E S S I N G P
A R S H M S P S E C D K S E T
G M P S I B L I O E V I L O A
A A A N I R A A P Y T Z E L H
R I A D Y R M L E E S T E A I
L M O K E D A E A L F A C S N
I A U L D I I H N O I Z U S I
C S H S I P R E U M S T A C A
S S I E T S R A T A H L S H E
A M T O D A Y I S C S G U U E
U O S T A U R N A A A D L T G
C J I V E C R D U U U S U N E
E O X T R E U A C G C C Z E F
L A V P U H C T E K E O E Y R
```

FISH SAUCE
GARLIC SAUCE
GUACAMOLE
HARISSA
HUMMUS
KETCHUP
MADEIRA SAUCE
MANIS
MAYONNAISE
MOJO
MUSTARD
OLIVE OIL
PADANG
PEANUT SAUCE
PESTO
ROUX
SALSA
SAMBAL
SOY SAUCE
TABASCO
TAHINI
TZATZIKI
ZULU SAUCE

AIOLI
CHUTNEY
CURRY
DAPUR
DIP SAUCE
DRESSING

FRIENDS?

What do the following words have in common?

CROWD COAT BOARD BURDEN BITE DOSE ABUNDANT

★★ Keep Going

Start on a blank square of your choice and connect as many blank squares as possible with one single continuous line. You can only connect squares along vertical and horizontal lines. You must continue the connecting line up until the next obstacle, i.e., the rim of the box, a black square or a square that has already been used. You can change direction at any obstacle you meet. Each square can be used only once. The number of blank squares that will be left unused is marked in the upper square. There is more than one solution. We show only one solution.

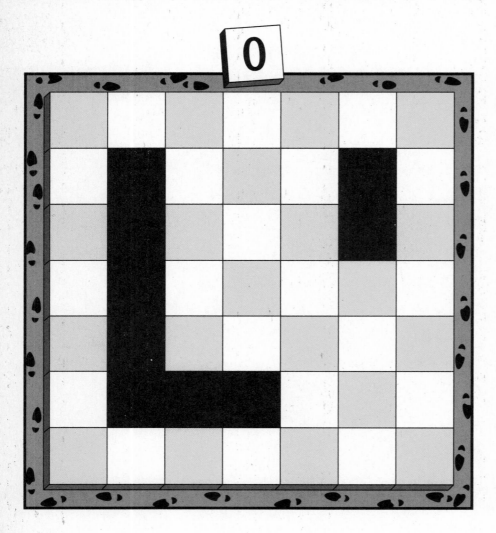

UNCANNY TURN

Rearrange the letters of the phrase below to form a cognate anagram, one which is related or connected in meaning to the original phrase. The answer can be one or more words.

RATE MY LIFE

★ Women Writers by Michele Sayer

ACROSS

1 Vishnu has four
5 Winfrey in *Beloved*
10 Cracked, as a door
14 Borscht ingredient
15 Lorna ___ cookies
16 Neck region
17 *Giant* novelist
19 Hydroxyl compound
20 Out-of-towners
21 *Twelfth Night* is one
23 Play horseshoes
24 Roman senate
25 Bette's *Little Foxes* role
28 Minute particle
31 *The Vampire Diaries* heroine
32 Cellar stock
33 Sexennial number
34 Bump on ___
35 Is a rat
36 "Quickly!" in the ER
37 Fallen space station
38 Ibsen's Gabler
39 "Hear no evil, ___ evil ..."
40 Orange sections
42 Of spring
43 Terra
44 Sun-dried
45 Time sharer, e.g.
47 Funnelform flora
51 Wife of Esau
52 Roderick Alleyn's creator
54 Trig function
55 The Pet Rock was one
56 Fawn over
57 Danson and Turner
58 Double-faulted
59 City near Tulsa

DOWN

1 Be a partner in crime
2 Kitchen face-lift
3 Pop-up list
4 Kind of track gate
5 Ukrainian port
6 Cities with wharves
7 Burgles
8 French donkey
9 Hydra killer
10 Lacking strength
11 *Pride and Prejudice* author
12 Footless animal
13 Put your money (on)
18 "On The Bound" singer Apple
22 Minerals
24 Cuban line dance
25 Bawls (out)
26 *Ice Age 3* mammoth
27 *Consuelo* novelist
28 Cares
29 Tarzan's vine
30 Sing the praises of
32 Shoebox info
35 San Quentin term
36 Suitor's song
38 "I've had it up to ___!"
39 Truth ___
41 Prepares spuds
42 Interdicted
44 Take possession of
45 Hindmost
46 *Desperate Housewives* divorcee
47 Early *Tonight Show* host
48 Club for Yani Tseng
49 Italian wine province
50 Took off
53 "I'm mad!"

★★★ Sudoku

Fill in the grid so that each row, each column and each 3 x 3 frame contains every number from 1 to 9.

4	7	9		1				2
3	5	6						
2							9	3
	9		2		1		4	
1		8	3	7	9		5	6
	7				4			9
8			1			6		5
						3		7
					8			

SANDWICH

What three-letter word belongs between the word on the left and the word on the right, so that the first and second word, and the second and third word, each form a common compound word or phrase?

MASS _ _ _ LESS

★★★ Sport Maze

Draw the shortest way from the ball to the goal. You can only move along vertical and horizontal lines, not along diagonal lines. The figure on each square indicates the number of squares the ball must be moved in the same direction. You can change direction at each stop.

3	4	1	5	1	4
1	2	●	3	0	1
2	3	0	3	4	1
5	1	1	3	1	2
1	4	1	4	1	5
3	5	5	2	4	2

CHANGE ONE, CHANGE ANOTHER

Change one letter in the first word to create a second word, then change one letter in the second word to create a third word which will become the final word by changing one letter. There may be more than one possible answer.

SEAT ➡ _ _ _ _ ➡ _ _ _ _ ➡ MELT

★ How Sweet It Is! by John M. Samson

ACROSS

1 "Name of the Game" group
5 Hold on tight
10 Invitation letters
14 Little Bo
15 1984 #1 hit by Lionel Richie
16 Missing from formation
17 Ike Clanton's foe
18 iPad letters
19 Honduras seaside city
20 "Want To" duo
22 "Grace Before Meat" painter
23 Used-car worry
24 Israeli port on the Gulf of Aqaba
25 Ponzi ___
28 2011 Super Bowl winner
32 Ralston of *127 Hours*
33 In the Land of Nod
35 Pie ___ mode
36 1983 Streisand film
38 Letterman's list number
39 ___ *With Love* (1967)
41 Lay eyes on
42 Aphrodite's love
45 Fasten
46 2012 London athlete
48 Bridal paths
50 Level, in Britain
51 Mine entrance
52 Bonnie's partner in crime
54 *Uncle Buck* star
59 Diane in *Chinatown*
60 Sidewalk show
61 "Ta-ta!"
62 Not windward
63 Pizarro's victims
64 Singer k.d.
65 Michael of "Star Trek: TNG"
66 Abacus counters
67 Morales in *Rapa Nui*

DOWN

1 *Rise of the Planet of the ___* (2011)
2 Boyfriend
3 Arctic Ocean hazard
4 Easy to grasp
5 First Family member in 2000
6 Paul in *American Graffiti*
7 Pianist Feinberg
8 Came home feet first
9 Khmer Rouge leader Pot
10 Wicker stick
11 Spaghetti sauce herb
12 Rat cousin
13 Blueprint
21 Pirate potable
22 Ended an all-nighter
24 Sneaker width
25 Approval
26 Basket for bass
27 *Dr. No* heroine
28 Friendship 7 astronaut
29 Santoni in *Dirty Harry*
30 '60s dress style
31 NFL stats
34 Peloponnesian porch
37 Gap in time
40 Stumbling block
43 Quit, as an engine
44 Blue state
47 Tick off
49 Caesar's 98
51 Yet to come
52 Wearing
53 *Le Roi d'Ys* composer
54 Miss Marple
55 Oceanic killer
56 Peeples and Vardalos
57 Delany in *Body of Proof*
58 Catcher for Whitey
60 Eve's origin

★ Word Sudoku

Complete the grid so that each row, each column and each 3 x 3 frame contains the nine letters from the black box below. The hidden nine-letter word is in the diagonal from top left to bottom right.

AEINOQRST

DELETE ONE

Delete one letter from IMPLY STARS and find a lifeline.

★★ BrainSnack®—Row Your Boat

How many people are in one skiff?

CONNECT TWO

An oxymoron is a combination of seemingly contradictory or incongruous words, such as "science fiction"(science means "knowledge or study dealing with facts or truth" while fiction means "an imagined or invented creation"). Connect the words with meanings that oppose each other and make oxymorons.

GLOBAL	PREGNANT
ALMOST	VILLAGE
FORGOTTEN	WHISPER
LOUD	MEMORIES

★ Alley Talk by Tim Wagner

ACROSS

1 Minstrel poet
5 Epps and Sharif
10 Margarita glass rim coater
14 Ancient lyre
15 Infant ailment
16 Others, to Ovid
17 Start conducting
20 Important global crop
21 How stir-fry is often served
22 Tolkien tree giant
23 Popular pop (with 60 Across)
24 Airships
28 Matter of little relevance
32 Bed of roses
33 *Legend of the Guardians* owl
34 Jim Bakker's former gp.
35 Share proceeds evenly
39 Spanish she-bear
40 Tibiae
41 Talking horse of Narnia
42 Like safety glass
44 Newsmen of yore
46 Cézanne summers
47 Moreover
48 Spanish wife
51 Titleholder
56 Pursued with deep pockets
58 Shania Twain's "___ Feel Like a Woman!"
59 Like Clive Barker's stories
60 See 23 Across
61 "Tell Mama" singer James
62 Baseball Hall-of-Famer Bobby
63 Sheepshank, e.g.

DOWN

1 British beer
2 Concerning
3 Golfer McIlroy
4 Smidgen
5 Oodles
6 Sermon on the ___
7 Site of Brenner Pass
8 Fabric dye brand
9 Grand Banks vessel
10 Native Israelis
11 Jai ___
12 Eagles' stadium (with "The")
13 Beach eroder
18 Hang on to
19 Brendan Fraser film ___ *Man*
23 Drum & bugle ___
24 Stupefy with drink
25 Pass by, as time
26 Religion of Pakistan
27 Pai ___ in *Kill Bill: Vol. 2*
28 Ad infinitum
29 Church riser
30 Verbalize
31 "Someone ___ Dream": Faith Hill
33 Acts skittish
36 Nagana carrier
37 Like screws
38 J. Edgar org.
43 "But will it play in ___?"
44 One using soft soap
45 Caper
47 "... ___ finest hour": Churchill
48 Cullen family matriarch
49 Small fight
50 Huff and puff
51 Apple discard
52 1/4 bushel
53 Privy to
54 Norway capital
55 Apple-pie order
57 Modern prefix

★ Binairo

Complete the grid with zeros and ones until there are 6 zeros and 6 ones in every row and every column. No more than two of the same number can be next to or under each other. Rows or columns with exactly the same content are not allowed. There is only one valid solution.

0							0		1		
			1	0						1	
		0						0			
					0			1			
		0						0			
1			1			1				1	
				1		1	0				
		0		1	1			0		0	
1		0									
		0							1	1	
	1						0			1	
		1		0	0		0	0			

LETTER LINE

Put a letter in each of the squares below to make a word which means "HELPFUL." These numbered clues refer to other words which can be made from the whole.

5 2 10 8 3 2 CAT; 3 6 4 7 2 RELATIVE; 5 9 1 10 2 STORY;
5 4 3 7 2 SEPARATING WALL; 7 9 1 6 3 HOME AWAY FROM HOME

1	2	3	4	5	6	7	8	9	10

★ Spot the Differences

Find the nine differences in the image on the right.

BLOCK ANAGRAM

Form the word that is described in the brackets with the letters above the grid. An extra letter is already in the right place.

TUNING (pursue for food or sport)

H					

★ Sporting Joes by Tim Wagner

ACROSS

1 Personal rights org.
5 Do a cakewalk
10 Play the predator
14 Provoke
15 This one and this one
16 Biopic about John Reed
17 Tracy Morrow, to the world
18 JUGS gun technology
19 *Picnic* playwright
20 Boxing Joes
23 Roman 1,101
24 Acquire a patina, say
25 Acquires
29 Last Supper figure
33 NHL MVP trophy
34 Zenith antonym
36 ___ up (angry)
37 Football Joes
41 ___ pro nobis
42 1973 Rolling Stones hit
43 Conscious of
44 Makes out
46 Keep bottled up
49 Part of ETA: Abbr.
50 Full circle?
51 Baseball Joes
60 Mediterranean port
61 Aquatic nymph
62 *East of Eden* director Kazan
63 Gala gathering
64 Kind of paper
65 El Paso school
66 No longer new
67 Reduced pain
68 Playbox filler

DOWN

1 Nutmeg husk
2 Chanel fragrance
3 "In ___ of flowers ..."
4 Eventual
5 Muscle injury
6 "Younger ___ Springtime"
7 Foxx who played Sanford
8 MQ-9 Reaper org.
9 Marylander
10 Game show giveaways
11 Baroque painter Guido
12 Ford model
13 Belgian river
21 Biol. or geol.
22 Where Socrates shopped
25 George Burns film
26 City near Montpelier

27 It's a good thing
28 Starts a run?
29 Terrestrial viper
30 Macduff, for one
31 Riga denizens
32 Societal values
35 Young Darth Vader
38 Shell's pearly layer
39 Captivate
40 Dream god
45 Part of ERA
47 Ducked
48 Irene's Roman counterpart
51 Vegetarian's protein source
52 Natural resources
53 Give stars to
54 Honshu shrine center
55 Goes flat, as a car battery

56 Red neck area
57 Utah ski resort
58 Creditor's claim
59 2001 Dennis Hopper film

★ Cage the Animals

Draw lines to completely divide up the grid into small squares with exactly one animal per square. The squares should not overlap.

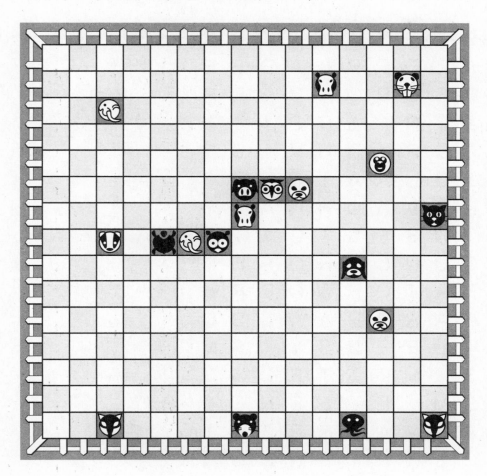

DOUBLETALK

Homophones are words that share the same pronunciation, no matter how they are spelled. If they are spelled differently then they are called heterographs. Find heterographs meaning:

AN ACUTE SHORTAGE and A WOMAN WITH A HABIT

★ Tools

All the words are hidden vertically, horizontally or diagonally—in both directions. The letters that remain unused form a sentence from left to right.

```
A  S  P  P  W  E  L  G  N  A  I  R  T  B  R
D  C  L  E  R  A  Z  O  R  B  L  A  D  E  E
R  I  A  N  R  O  S  C  R  O  W  B  A  R  P
I  S  N  K  G  E  T  N  W  A  S  G  I  J  A
L  S  E  H  C  L  D  R  I  C  H  V  I  S  R
L  O  R  C  E  I  O  N  A  A  I  S  A  P  C
W  R  E  N  C  H  T  V  A  C  H  N  A  L  S
I  S  L  U  D  T  H  S  E  S  T  C  A  I  T
M  S  U  P  P  O  U  N  D  E  R  O  E  E  P
P  E  R  F  O  R  A  T  O  R  W  C  R  R  L
R  S  T  E  K  C  A  R  B  R  A  W  L  S  U
U  E  R  A  F  I  L  E  E  E  S  Y  I  S  M
E  H  T  A  L  S  I  M  T  T  E  C  W  B
M  S  W  T  H  S  M  I  E  L  E  E  N  E  L
L  I  A  N  U  A  A  M  W  O  R  R  E  R  I
L  E  S  I  H  C  L  W  K  I  F  N  P  C  N
G  O  N  N  T  E  C  A  L  I  P  E  R  S  E
H  K  E  M  H  E  F  I  N  K  Y  T  T  U  P
```

HELMET
INK
JIGSAW
LATHE
METAL SAW
NAIL
PENCIL
PERFORATOR
PLANER
PLIERS
PLUMB LINE
POUNDER
PROTRACTOR
PUNCH
PUTTY KNIFE
RAZOR BLADE
RULER
SANDER
SCISSORS
SCRAPER
SCREWS
TRIANGLE
WRENCH
YARDSTICK

AWL	CHISEL	FILE
BRACKETS	CROWBAR	FRETSAW
CALIPERS	CUTTER	GLOVE
CHAIN SAW	DRILL	HAMMER

DELETE ONE

Delete one letter from ONE PAST INCOME and find fair reward.

★★ Sunny Weather

Where will the sun shine? With the knowledge that each arrow points to a place where a symbol should be, can you locate the sunny spots? The symbols cannot be next to each other vertically, horizontally or diagonally. A symbol cannot be placed on top of an arrow. We show one symbol.

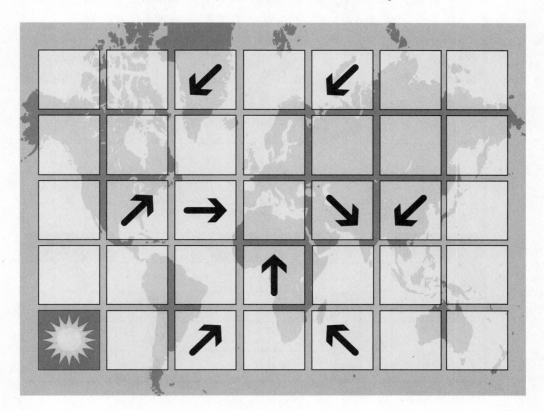

UNCANNY TURN

Rearrange the letters of the phrase below to form a cognate anagram, one which is related or connected in meaning to the original phrase. The answer can be one or more words.

ON SCALE OF SIN

★ There's Something About ... by Peggy O'Shea

ACROSS

1 Creator of Dogpatch
5 One of the out-crowd?
10 Sandler in *Jack and Jill*
14 Shrinking Asian sea
15 Give up voluntarily
16 Float up
17 Solo's soulmate
18 Suffix for the wealthy?
19 *Field of Dreams* setting
20 *Ordinary People* star
23 Tom Collins ingredient
24 R.E.M. record label
25 Ends up
29 Bobolink
33 Off-Broadway award
34 ___ potato
36 Latin 101 word
37 James Jones novel (with *The*)
41 "It's cold!"
42 Took part in a regatta
43 Behind schedule
44 Add haphazardly
46 Membrane permeation
49 Bard's nightfall
50 St. Anthony's cross
51 Union request?
59 Cover up
60 Divide up
61 Don Imus, familiarly
62 Road to Roma
63 Take as spoils
64 Bigeye fish
65 Open carriage
66 Adventured
67 Broadway muggers

DOWN

1 Cool-headed
2 Geometry calculation
3 Part of a full house
4 Theater fan
5 Wade of the NBA
6 Mourn out loud
7 Wexford locale
8 Unceasingly
9 Tarnish
10 Like a song
11 Fashion designer
12 "... even ___ speak"
13 "Give ___ break!"
21 Allen in *Wild Hogs*
22 Straight: Comb. form
25 Strikes out
26 Chicago film critic
27 Wispy clouds
28 Ridicule

29 Go one better
30 Eastern priests
31 Priceless violin
32 "The Barrel-Organ" poet
35 ___ and the same
38 Rube
39 Long spar
40 "Ta-da!," e.g.
45 Salad stalk
47 Spoke
48 Damage slightly
51 Also starring
52 Flash of brilliance
53 Olive genus
54 Suffix for gland
55 Pawn to king's bishop 3, e.g.
56 Village People hit
57 What to call a lady

58 Calls it quits
59 ___ *for Homicide*: Grafton

★ Kakuro

Each number in a black area is the sum of the numbers that you have to enter in the next empty boxes. The empty boxes that make up the sum are called a run. The sum of the across run is written above the diagonal in the black area and the sum of the down run is written below the diagonal. Runs can only contain the numbers 1 through 9 and each number in a run can only be used once. The gray boxes only contain odd numbers and the white only even numbers.

DELETE ONE

Delete one letter from PROD IN COURT and find a reason to be there.

★★★ BrainSnack®—Winner?

Which number should replace the question marks to know the distance from the winning boccie ball to the aim ball?

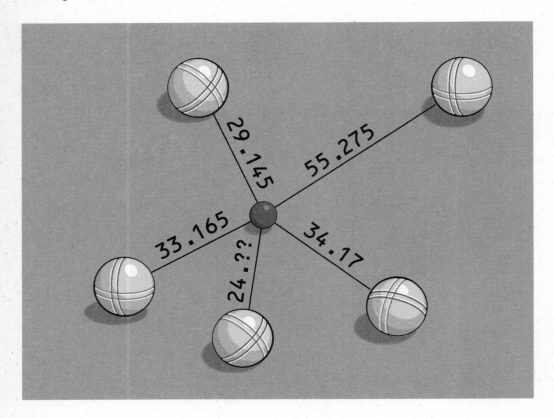

CHANGELINGS

Each of the three lines of letters below spells a word that has a theatrical connection, but the letters have been mixed up. Four letters from the first word are now in the third line, four letters from the third word are in the second line and four letters from the second word are in the first line. The remaining letters are in their original places. What are the words?

U O O D L I G U Y S
P N F E R S T M D G
F E R T O R H I N T

★ Presidential Nicknames by Don Law

ACROSS

1 It's as good as a nod
5 Jog
9 Carved memorial
14 Coldplay's "___ Love"
15 Protagonist
16 Mexican film award
17 "His Accidency" president
19 U.S.-born Japanese
20 Paper-folding art
21 Rash symptom
23 Schlock
25 Reclined
26 Hasbro action figures
29 "Keeper of sheep" in Genesis
31 Hockey's ___ trick
34 Ansel of photography
35 Pond denizens
36 Eastern sash
37 Fordham team
38 Locked book
39 Exercised in the water
40 French tea
41 Dovetail part
42 Section
43 Santa's syllables
44 Pen sound
45 Bay of Bengal city
46 2009 *American Idol* winner Allen
48 Skip a syllable
50 *Carrie* director Brian
53 Hailing from Haifa
57 Love to pieces
58 "Long Tom" president
60 Bay or fjord
61 Against
62 Attorney Geragos
63 Fermented rice brews
64 Musician's pause
65 On-tap serving

DOWN

1 *Barney Miller* cop
2 "Are you ___ out?"
3 Soda since the 1920s
4 Monarchies
5 Aromatic herbs
6 Object of veneration
7 Assay sample
8 1 mmHg pressure
9 Summer attire
10 "If I Had a Hammer" singer Lopez
11 "Kansas Cyclone" president
12 Wine waste
13 Certain Ivy Leaguers
18 Weight factors
22 Melancholy poem
24 Bar activity, perhaps
26 "Burning Bridges" singer Brooks
27 Twin Falls site
28 "Napoleon of the Stump" president
30 Foaled
32 Philippine banana tree
33 L.A. newspaper
35 Sawyer's pal
38 Voltaire's belief
39 Body heat?
41 Privies
42 Barcelona dad
45 Fish out of water
47 ___ show (street carnival)
49 Impromptu rides
50 Awards night platform
51 Tracy's *Hairspray* mom
52 Slightly open
54 Father of the Edomites
55 Feudal bigwig
56 Signs on the dotted line
59 Phoenix–Philly dir.

★★ Keep Going

Start on a blank square of your choice and connect as many blank squares as possible with one single continuous line. You can only connect squares along vertical and horizontal lines. You must continue the connecting line up until the next obstacle, i.e., the rim of the box, a black square or a square that has already been used. You can change direction at any obstacle you meet. Each square can be used only once. The number of blank squares that will be left unused is marked in the upper square. There is more than one solution. We show only one solution.

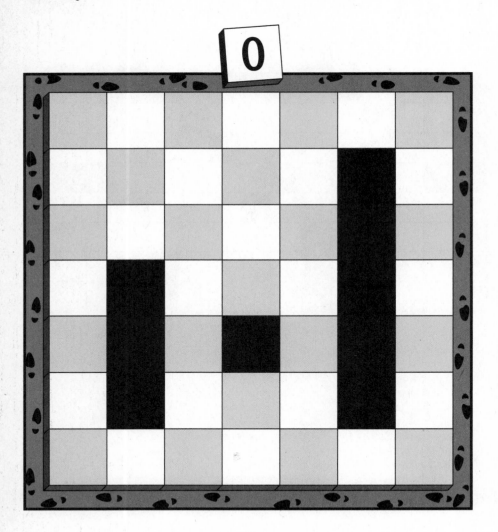

REPOSITION PREPOSITION

Unscramble FEW RETICENT HERO and find a three-word preposition.

★ Sudoku

Fill in the grid so that each row, each column and each 3 x 3 frame contains every number from 1 to 9.

			9					
	5							
		3	2			6		
			8	7				
3		5		6		8		
	7			2	3		5	9
6		9	5	8	1		4	
5	2			4				
7	4			9		3	8	5

ONE LETTER LESS OR MORE

The word on the right side contains the letters of the word on the left side plus or minus the letter in the middle. One letter is already in the right place.

B E D R O O M S -S ☐ O ☐ ☐ ☐ ☐

★ Diana's Realm by John McCarthy

ACROSS

1 Twitter mascot
5 Gripping gadget
10 Masterstroke
14 Mine, in Montreal
15 Renault of the 1970s
16 Sacramento arena
17 Black-and-white treats
20 Powers of *Hart to Hart*
21 Dogmata
22 Horned Alpine beast
23 Futurist
24 Unearthed
27 Goes a-courtin'?
28 Cousin of a lemur
31 Ramshackle residence
32 Hydrochloric ___
33 Suffix with cell
34 Beethoven piano piece
37 "I'm ___, boss!"
38 It's given at birth
39 Goes off on a mad tangent
40 Gondolier's pole
41 Jackson 5 hairstyle
42 Eric Knight's collie
43 Hawkish deity
44 *Art of the Fugue* composer
45 Midfielder's sport
48 Survives
52 Lunar resident?
54 Auxiliary
55 Glacial ridge
56 Franc's replacement
57 Takes off
58 Speed trap
59 Barrymore in *Scream*

DOWN

1 Scrooge-like utterances
2 "___ my wit's end!"
3 It's played on a stage
4 Bashful
5 Made an exact duplicate
6 11th-century Pope
7 Facial spots
8 *JAG* heroine
9 Gate
10 Possum player
11 Lake bordering Ontario
12 Served a winner
13 Let fly
18 AT&T's nickname
19 Metal rock group
23 Honeymoon lodgings
24 Al Capp cartoon character
25 City southeast of Mumbai
26 French 101 verb
27 Yiddish dunce
28 Simpson and Dershowitz
29 LuPone of musicals
30 Remove graphite
32 Seaweed gels
33 Devoid of guilt
35 Hellish
36 Divine revelation
41 Territory
42 Suds
43 Pinnacles
44 Badlands hill
45 Prewedding party
46 Cincinnati's river
47 Hand over
48 Billfold filler
49 Bitter
50 Ripped
51 Mount Fuji cap
53 Flatow of *Science Friday*

★ Futoshiki

Fill in the 5 x 5 grid with the numbers from 1 to 5 once per row and column, while following the greater than/lesser than symbols shown. There is only one valid solution that can be reached through logic and clear thinking alone!

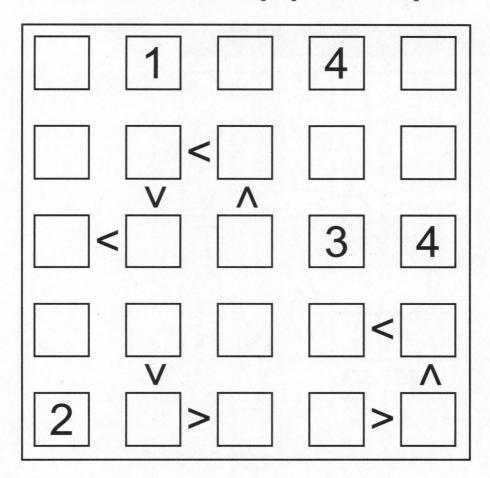

DOODLE PUZZLE

A doodle puzzle is a combination of images, letters and/or numbers that represent a word or a concept. If you cannot solve a doodle puzzle, do not look at the answer right away. Think hard—and outside the box.

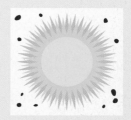

★ Word Sudoku

Complete the grid so that each row, each column and each 3 x 3 frame contains
the nine letters from the black box below. The hidden nine-letter word is in the
diagonal from top left to bottom right.

A F L N O R T U V

					O			
	N	F						
U	R			A				V
N			R	F				T
L					A		O	
			T	V	N	R		
A			F	R		V		
	T					L		
O		U		V		T	A	

LETTERBLOCKS

Move the letterblocks around so that words
are formed on top and below that you can
associate with clothing.

★★★ BrainSnack®—Home Port

Which letter is missing in the name of the last port that the yachtsman will enter at the end of his voyage?

NEWPORT
EVERSOR
VOVINO
ORLEMAN
RIMIN?

DOUBLETALK

Homophones are words that share the same pronunciation, no matter how they are spelled. If they are spelled differently then they are called heterographs. Find heterographs meaning:

TO REDUCE and SOMETHING TAUGHT

★ 36 Across by Kelly Lynch

ACROSS
1 Mud dauber
5 Homer epic
10 Postmortem notice
14 Foot part
15 Polonium discoverer
16 Singsong reply
17 Where Greek met Greek
18 Small, rounded hill
19 Creative thought
20 Kind of blue
22 Kind of blue
23 Less anxious
24 Cezanne or Gauguin
26 Dory mover
27 Trade
31 Come about
34 What statistics give
35 So last year
36 Complete surprise/ TITLE
40 Artist Yoko
41 Bleating belles
42 Certain con
43 Strong coffee
46 Super Bowl org.
47 *Commedia dell'___*
48 Comfort stations
52 Rock bottom
55 Kind of blue
56 Olympian hawk
57 Icelandic inlet
59 Chocolate cookie
60 Turpitude
61 Conical residence
62 Disney clownfish
63 Tibetan oxen
64 Judge played by Stallone
65 Make a move

DOWN
1 Strands of smoke
2 Cavern, in poetry
3 Search high and low
4 Bring to an end gradually
5 More disgusting
6 Kind of eclipse
7 Do a pressing job
8 Be in a bad way
9 Marina ___ Rey
10 Maryland's state bird
11 It might be heavenly
12 White-flowering shrub
13 River duck
21 Wolf down
22 Daiquiri ingredient
24 Annie in *Ghostbusters*
25 *The Joy Luck Club* nanny
27 Carved medallion
28 Liesl von Trapp's love
29 Sleuth's find
30 River that joins the Fulda
31 Clarinet cousin
32 Time servers
33 Hoofbeat
34 Look for water
37 "No ___ for the weary"
38 Pixyish
39 Huge amounts
44 Poker bluffs, at times
45 Flub
46 Showed agreement
48 Ready to hit the hay
49 White marsh bird
50 Essay in a school notebook
51 Scrooch down
52 Kind of blue
53 "Casta diva," e.g.
54 Dealer's handful
55 Act depressed
57 Bouquet delivery co.
58 Suffix for cash

★ Cage the Animals

Draw lines to completely divide up the grid into small squares with exactly one animal per square. The squares should not overlap.

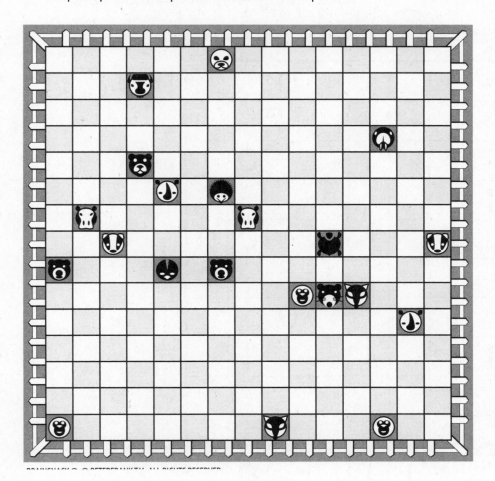

FRIENDS?

What do the following words have in common?

HOUSE GROW SULK ACHIEVE DOORS PATIENTS

★ Binairo

Complete the grid with zeros and ones until there are 5 zeros and 6 ones in every row and every column. No more than two of the same number can be next to or under each other. Rows or columns with exactly the same content are not allowed. There is only one valid solution.

				I				O		
					I			O	I	
			I							
								O	O	
		I		I		I			O	
I	O						O			
		I			I			I		
I	O									
		O	O				I		I	
I	O		O	I	I			O		

CONNECT TWO

An oxymoron is a combination of seemingly contradictory or incongruous words, such as "science fiction"(science means "knowledge or study dealing with facts or truth" while fiction means "an imagined or invented creation"). Connect the words with meanings that oppose each other and make oxymorons.

ANXIOUS	SHRIMP
JUMBO	SHADE
LIGHT	PILOT
AUTO	PATIENT

★★★ Chairman of the Board by John M. Samson

ACROSS

1 Twosome
5 Pole of Highland games
10 Foundling
14 Fairytale opener
15 Light of foot
16 Not pro
17 1958 Frank Sinatra hit
19 "___ a Kick Out of You"
20 Strives to match
21 Comes out with
23 Remnant
24 Oliver's porridge
25 Votes against
26 Not abstract
29 Less than always
32 She played the 10 in *10*
33 Desire
34 Cowardly Lion portrayer
35 Cryptic
36 Ward off
37 Eggs
38 Atkinson in *Mr. Bean*
39 Doesn't die out
40 Storekeeper, e.g.
42 Palindromic parent
43 Boxer's seat
44 "Everybody ___ Cha Cha Cha": Cooke
48 They earned their wings
50 Nelly Furtado song
51 *Alias* Emmy winner Lena
52 1966 Frank Sinatra hit
54 Under lock and key
55 MacDowell in *Beauty Shop*
56 Feed the kitty
57 Starry-___ idealist
58 *Star Wars: Episode I* director
59 Bela's *Son of Frankenstein* role

DOWN

1 Strength
2 Japanimation
3 Metrical accent
4 Easy chair
5 Prickly pear
6 Jibe
7 Hate crime cause
8 Brownie
9 Went back
10 One to tip
11 1958 Frank Sinatra hit
12 Anatomical duct
13 Is the right size
18 Modeled
22 Sherwood Forest friar
24 Bridge maven
26 Closet wood
27 Pavilion
28 Puts a halt to
29 Swan genus
30 Pet, slangily
31 1966 Frank Sinatra hit
32 Carpenter's peg
35 Gargantuan
36 Fallback jump shot
38 Real cutup
39 Melbourne's Rod ___ Arena
41 Expiated
42 Presentees
44 Female vampire
45 "Fields of Gold" singer
46 Fifty minutes past
47 Directive
48 It's sometimes struck
49 "Now ___ me down ..."
50 2600, to Caesar
53 Burma's first prime minister

★ BrainSnack®—Snakeskin

Which color (1-4) should replace the question mark?

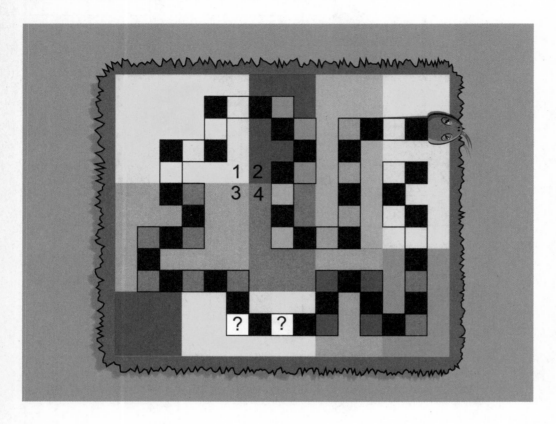

SANDWICH

What four-letter word belongs between the word on the left and the word on the right, so that the first and second word, and the second and third word, each form a common compound word or phrase?

PASS _ _ _ _ PLAY

★ Actions

All the words are hidden vertically, horizontally or diagonally—in both directions. The letters that remain unused form a sentence from left to right.

```
K N O C K P U L L C F E T C H
C E B V E E A E R O Y T O Y P
E E E W D X O S F V A K U C E
H T Y I A D A I S E O O C N K
C U C M R L E M A R N O H S A
S E N A O M K S I N G C E T T
D H W T N I P C O N Q U E R N
S I E R E S C U E S E L E C T
G H V V T G W O N C T H I E P
E S O O H C N E N I E R S A O
H L M O R N P A R E S R F O F
S R M I T C D N H G H T E H
U E A C T A E J S C N D I X T
P C K A N B E U D E S I G P N
A T E A D T R M A S U N D L E
E R A S E B U P R S T A N A D
A B L E B P E R A P M O C I E
H T L U A S S A N A V I O N R
```

COMPARE
CONQUER
~~COOK~~
~~COVER~~
DANCE
DECIDE
DIVORCE
DRAW
ERASE
~~EXAMINE~~
EXPLAIN
FAIL
~~FETCH~~
~~HUNT~~
~~JUMP~~
~~KNOCK~~
LOVE
MOVE
OBEY
PASS
~~PULL~~
PUNISH
PUSH
RESCUE
SELECT
SHOOT
SING
SPEAK
TAKE
TOUCH
TURN
~~WALK~~

ANSWER
ASSAULT
~~BRUSH~~
CHANGE
CHECK
CHOOSE

UNCANNY TURN

Rearrange the letters of the phrase below to form a cognate anagram, one which is related or connected in meaning to the original phrase. The answer can be one or more words.

A FLARING END

★★ 1950s No. 1 Hits by Michele Sayer

ACROSS

1 Carte du jour
5 Dances
10 Steel girder
14 Cat in *Peter and the Wolf*
15 *Adam Bede* novelist
16 Loch Ness Monster, for one
17 1955 Chuck Berry hit
19 Soccer's "Black Pearl"
20 Wouldn't take no for an answer
21 Where Mecca is
23 "...____ o'clock scholar"
24 Board for nails
25 Spake as a snake
28 Apple pastries
31 Pays a stud fee?
32 "Crazy" singer Patsy
33 Illumined
34 A ton
35 Street talk
36 Bridge coup
37 Touchy game
38 "____ Love": Brad Paisley
39 Assembly of witches
40 Least likely to forgive
42 Ohio city
43 House of Lords group
44 U. military group
45 Red-eyed polecat
47 Kangaroo and Kidd
51 *Winnie ____ Pu*
52 1955 hit by the Crew-Cuts
54 Tennis star Monfils
55 Mrs. Gorbachev
56 Skye in *Gas Food Lodging*
57 Weaver's reed
58 Noisy shoe
59 Racing team

DOWN

1 *La Bohème* heroine
2 Welsh form of John
3 Ayes' antitheses
4 Fair
5 Sang loudly (with "out")
6 *Annie Hall* director
7 Made stuff up
8 Either of the Chaneys
9 Hot under the collar
10 Disclose
11 1957 Everly Brothers hit
12 Gudrun's husband
13 Poseidon's mom
18 Will in *Blue Bloods*
22 Astrolabe plate
24 Brockovich et al.
25 "____ la vista, baby!"
26 Like Machu Picchu
27 1959 Lloyd Price hit
28 Lester of bluegrass
29 All worked up
30 Court employee
32 Mail grade
35 Tax reducers
36 Like cinder cones
38 Become sleepy
39 Terra ____
41 Hardly ever
42 Classy chapeau
44 *Midnight Cowboy* role
45 Newton fruits
46 Tel Aviv carrier
47 Place for corn
48 Frankenstein's assistant
49 Hawaiian goose
50 Killed
53 Small battery

★★ BrainSnack®—Choose Your Cheese

The mouse has already collected four cheese cubes. Which cheese cube (1–6) will it collect now?

DELETE ONE

Delete one letter from GRIP ON SEAT and find a place without gum.

★★★ Sudoku

Fill in the grid so that each row, each column and each 3 x 3 frame contains every number from 1 to 9.

4	9		8			7	5	
						6	1	
	5	6	1	7			9	2
5		9		1			4	7
7				9			6	
1		3		4				
		8			5			
			6					
	4			3		1		

END GAME

The words you are seeking all have the letters END in them in the position indicated. When you have found all of the answers, from the clues on the right, one column will reveal the END GAME word which is not hard to beat.

_ _ E N D _ _	Corrected
E N D _ _ _ _	One who bears or sustains
_ E N D _ _ _	Auctions
E N D _ _ _ _	Unique to a defined location

★★ 1960s No. 1 Hits by Michele Sayer

ACROSS

1 Stately shade providers
5 The first to stab Caesar
10 Entrance for a collier
14 Bounder
15 Take heat from?
16 Scheme
17 1963 Lesley Gore hit
19 Covering for an iPod
20 Neighbor of Kenya
21 Places to putter around?
23 Aliases
24 Sky: Comb. form
25 Buffalo skaters
28 Scandalous
31 "When ___ said and done"
32 Spa amenity
33 "Turn to Stone" group
34 Booming
35 Father's Day gift
36 Compos mentis
37 Suffix for prop
38 Florida city
39 Stable bedding
40 Unfolds
42 Sobieski of *Joan of Arc*
43 Ruling class
44 Easily carved gem
45 Lifers, e.g.
47 *The ___ Inferno* (1974)
51 "Please respond"
52 1961 Pat Boone hit
54 Hosea, in the Douay Bible
55 *The Mosquito Coast* hero
56 Basilica area
57 Citi Field team
58 Noted consumer advocate
59 Eat like a rat

DOWN

1 Lake in HOMES
2 NFL Hall-of-Famer Ronnie
3 Husky command
4 Somewhat parched
5 Spots of tea
6 *Solar Barque* author Nin
7 *Water for Elephants* novelist Gruen
8 Old PC monitor
9 "Baby Baby" singer
10 Detective Lupin
11 1962 Gene Chandler hit
12 "The proof ___ the pudding"
13 Sawbucks
18 Pairs oxen
22 Wolf who adopted Mowgli
24 *Star Trek* crew member
25 Waldorf ___
26 Unparalleled
27 1963 Bobby Vinton hit
28 "Red ___ in the Sunset"
29 Arm bones
30 *My Fair Lady* composer
32 Silhouette
35 Haggis eater
36 At the wheel
38 *The Reader* actress Lena
39 Passover meal
41 Marries in secret
42 Barrister
44 Foster in *The Beaver*
45 Starting at
46 Latin 101 verb
47 Finked on
48 Name of six tsars
49 St. Petersburg river
50 Shot up
53 Suffix for pay

★ Word Sudoku

Complete the grid so that each row, each column and each 3 x 3 frame contains the nine letters from the black box below. The hidden nine-letter word is in the diagonal from top left to bottom right.

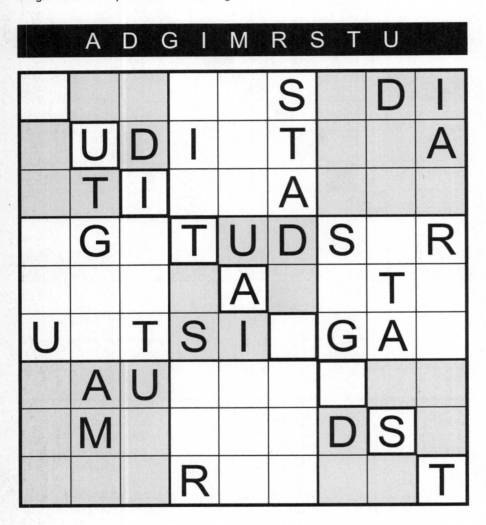

A D G I M R S T U

BLOCK ANAGRAM

Form the words that are described in the brackets with the letters above the grid. Extra letters are already in the right place.

MINI MONT BLANC *(outdoor sport)*

☐ ☐ **U** ☐ ☐ ☐ ☐   ☐ ☐ **I** ☐ ☐ ☐ **G**

★★★ Sport Maze

Draw the shortest way from the ball to the goal. You can only move along vertical and horizontal lines, not along diagonal lines. The figure on each square indicates the number of squares the ball must be moved in the same direction. You can change direction at each stop.

1	3	4	4	3	2
5	3	3	1	4	1
1	4	2	1	3	4
2	4	3	0	3	3
3	3	1	1	2	
1	4	5	1	2	1

DELETE ONE

Delete one letter from SETS HARD AREAS and find sand.

★★ 1970s No. 1 Hits by Michele Sayer

ACROSS

1 Jason's ship
5 Fantasize
10 Ski lift
14 Chucklehead
15 Utah mountains
16 Folk singer Guthrie
17 1970 hit by the Carpenters
19 Unassisted
20 Miss from Cadiz
21 Dork
23 Falsities
24 Black Forest spa
25 They're out of this world
28 Gargantuan
31 Judo sashes
32 Boxcar hoppers
33 Charlottesville col.
34 Play the wolf
35 Deadly African snake
36 Like fine Scotch
37 Light pat
38 Mudville slugger
39 Frighten
40 Ingredients
42 Red suit
43 Lingerie item
44 Half-moon tide
45 "Das Klagende Lied" composer
47 Lisbon locale
51 "... ___ saw Elba"
52 1971 Carole King hit
54 Arctic seabird
55 Major French river
56 Blondie drummer Burke
57 Sailing
58 Takes second
59 Olive genus

DOWN

1 Basics
2 Othello, e.g.
3 Bullyboy
4 Archaic
5 Import taxes
6 Runs rampant
7 "The Memory of Trees" singer
8 From ___ Z
9 Hawaiian volcano
10 Has a spoonful
11 1971 Rolling Stones hit
12 "___ want for Christmas ..."
13 Carrot, for one
18 Moran and Gray
22 Nuptial exchanges
24 Riggs of tennis
25 Living quarters

26 Type of holiday
27 1970 Jackson 5 hit
28 Hails (from)
29 Forestall
30 Does dock work
32 Like Harvard's pudding
35 Big baboon
36 Cliff-diving Mexican resort
38 Surrender formally
39 NATO's former kin
41 Mercouri in *Never On Sunday*
42 Chivalrous ones
44 U. of ___ Dame
45 "I ___ man with seven ..."
46 Bellicose god
47 23rd Greek letters
48 Chutzpah
49 To ___ (exactly)

50 "Champagne Tony" of golf
53 As well

★★★ BrainSnack®—Name That Dessert

The chef wants a new name for his dessert so he writes down a few logical variants. What will the last variant be?

DOUBLETALK

Homophones are words that share the same pronunciation, no matter how they are spelled. If they are spelled differently then they are called heterographs. Find heterographs meaning:

TO TOUCH ON A SUBJECT and WORN WITH A PIN

★ Sudoku Twin

Fill in the grid so that each row, each column and each 3 x 3 frame contains every number from 1 to 9. A sudoku twin is two connected 9 x 9 sudokus.

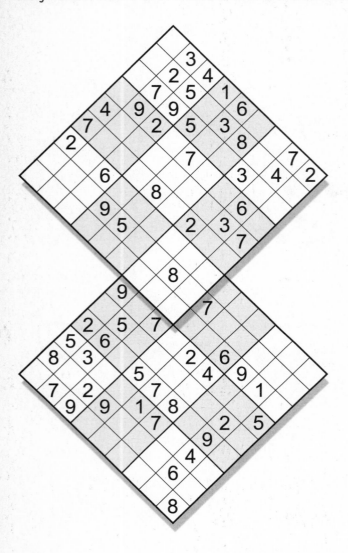

DOODLE PUZZLE

A doodle puzzle is a combination of images, letters and/or numbers that represent a word or a concept. If you cannot solve a doodle puzzle, do not look at the answer right away. Think hard—and outside the box.

DEEF

★★ 1980s No. 1 Hits by Michele Sayer

ACROSS

1 "A Boy Named Sue" singer
5 Puts into alignment
10 Boom partner
14 Skin cream additive
15 Detritus
16 Ronny Howard role
17 1983 Michael Jackson hit
19 "___ that something!"
20 Freeze in one's tracks
21 Do a favor
23 "Sure, why not?"
24 Lhasa apso, e.g.
25 Way to get in
28 Constructors
31 "When thou ___ alms ...": Matt. 6:3
32 Ray in the sea
33 Morse sound
34 Film composer Zimmer
35 ___ Doone cookies
36 Aaron Spelling's daughter
37 Leaf-peeping mo.
38 Little finger
39 Less
40 London pharmacists
42 Eliot's miser Silas
43 Path of travel
44 Teri in *Young Frankenstein*
45 Say "no"
47 Master copy
51 Youngest Greek god
52 1980 Dolly Parton hit
54 Has a malady
55 Inorganic salt
56 Nuptial vows
57 Ancient Persian
58 Geneva river
59 Insulting tip

DOWN

1 Vehicles for hire
2 Landed
3 Fly without a copilot
4 Like newborns
5 Twitter messages
6 Hindu royals
7 Worn
8 Timetable abbr.
9 Miss of Madrid
10 Seethed
11 1980 Diana Ross hit
12 Lift up one's voice
13 Head of France
18 Latin for "that is"
22 Banjo player Fleck
24 Bugs ___
25 Type of committee
26 Team leader
27 1981 J. Geils Band hit
28 Talks like Lassie
29 Sidewalk show
30 Bake eggs
32 Three-card game
35 Fan of talk radio
36 Fabulous
38 J.K. Rowling's Thicknesse
39 1996 Frances McDormand film
41 Creamy dessert
42 ___ d' (headwaiter)
44 Light you can go through
45 500 sheets
46 Perry's lake
47 Not fooled by
48 Pheasant brood
49 Stratford river
50 "___ we forget"
53 Suffix for boy

★★ Sunny Weather

Where will the sun shine? With the knowledge that each arrow points to
a place where a symbol should be, can you locate the sunny spots? The
symbols cannot be next to each other vertically, horizontally or diagonally.
A symbol cannot be placed on top of an arrow. We show one symbol.

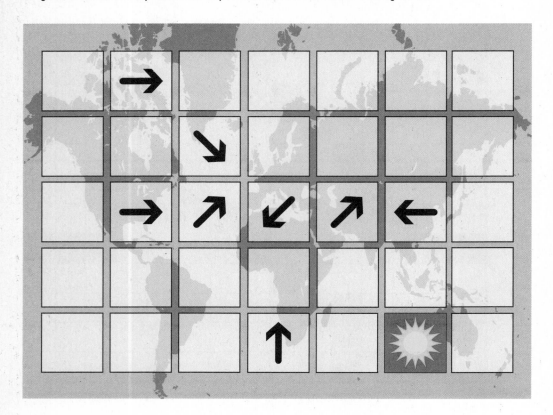

DELETE ONE

Delete one letter from SAND IDIOT and find a sum.

★★★ BrainSnack®—Olives

Which group of olives (1–6) isn't part of the series?

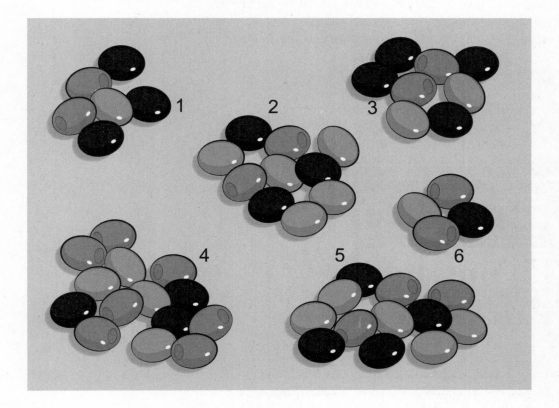

SANDWICH

What four-letter word belongs between the word on the left and the word on the right, so that the first and second word, and the second and third word, each form a common compound word or phrase?

PHOTO _ _ _ _ BOOK

★ Safe Code

To open the safe you have to replace the question mark with the correct figure. You can find this figure by determining the logical method behind the numbers shown. These methods can include calculation, inversion, repetition, chronological succession, forming ascending and descending series.

SAFE A08

LETTERBLOCKS

Move the letterblocks around so that words are formed on top and below that you can associate with health.

★★ Beer Belly by Tim Wagner

ACROSS

1 Pageantry
5 Queenly
10 Dick and Jane's dog
14 Native maid in India
15 Hirsch in *Milk*
16 Strong feeling
17 Slangy term for a lawyer
19 Bare it all
20 Spanish fortress
21 Sit and spin
23 Vice
24 Company dishes?
25 Categorize
28 Removed snow
31 Brimless cap
32 Tipperary's neighbor
33 Mendes in *Ghost Rider*
34 Moron
35 Crinkled cotton fabric
36 ___ Penh: Var.
37 Cleaned a plate
38 Responds to sun and water
39 Sondra in *Sudden Impact*
40 Shoals
42 Buffalo hide homes
43 Dirty rat
44 Hand, in Juárez
45 Barn sounds
47 Ant bear
51 Paul in *Anchorman*
52 Be on the mend
54 Orchestral tuner
55 *The Odd Couple* neatnik
56 Frost-flecked
57 Navigate
58 "Lovergirl" singer Marie
59 Laurel and Hardy personae

DOWN

1 Insect sensor
2 Court hearing
3 Wizard
4 Eliminate gradually
5 Make further corrections
6 Stampless correspondence
7 Data-entry acronym
8 Whole shebang
9 Winslow Homer's "On a ___"
10 Prone
11 Extent
12 S-shaped molding
13 Notify
18 French book
22 Take a bride
24 Leather leggings
25 Rand's ___ *Shrugged*
26 Kind of sayer
27 Snitched
28 Gobs
29 Arouse, as feelings
30 Titled ladies
32 Russell in *Robin Hood*
35 Logging saw
36 Puffy pastries
38 Flood the market
39 1987 French Open winner
41 Stinking rich
42 "___ Boom-De-Ay"
44 Expert
45 Facial hair
46 Grease job
47 French seraph
48 Large land mass
49 Mounties: Abbr.
50 Locksmith's stock
53 Ace, on the scorecard

★ Hourglass

Starting in the middle, each word in the top half has the letters of the word below it, plus a new letter, and each word in the bottom half has the letters of the word above it, plus a new letter.

(1) visible horizon
(2) satiny
(3) connections
(4) drop down

(5) tie together
(6) stench
(7) believes
(8) noble persons trained to arms and chivalry

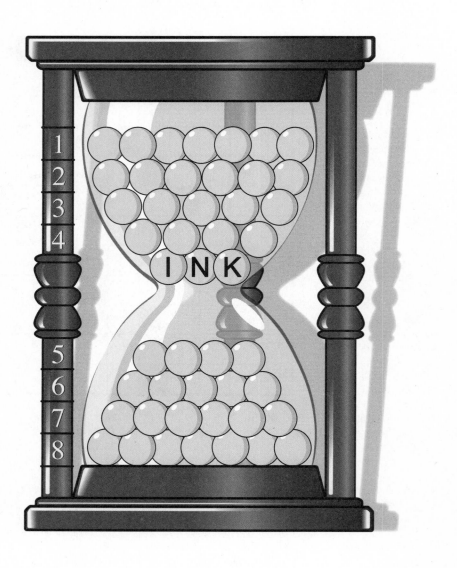

LETTERBLOCKS

Move the letterblocks around so that words are formed on top and below that you can associate with agriculture.

★★ Keep Going

Start on a blank square of your choice and connect as many blank squares as possible with one single continuous line. You can only connect squares along vertical and horizontal lines. You must continue the connecting line up until the next obstacle, i.e., the rim of the box, a black square or a square that has already been used. You can change direction at any obstacle you meet. Each square can be used only once. The number of blank squares that will be left unused is marked in the upper square. There is more than one solution. We show only one solution.

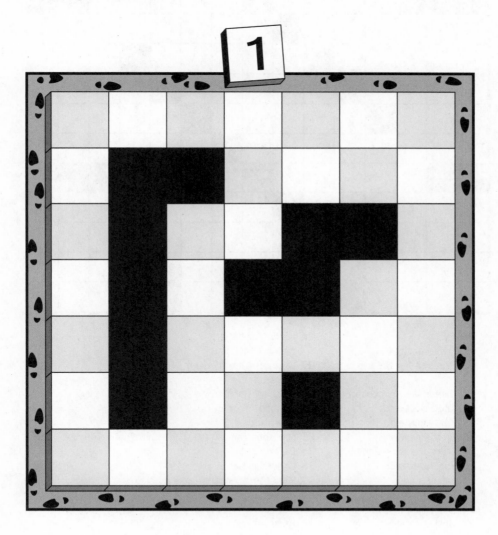

DELETE ONE

Delete one letter from HIRE CANDLES and find another light source.

★★ Diminutive by Cindy Wheeler

ACROSS

1 Roulette bet
5 County in Ireland
10 Island near Corsica
14 From Sinai to Shanghai
15 Benghazi locale
16 Currency of Iran
17 1971 Elton John hit
19 *Volsunga Saga* king
20 Smitten
21 Crunch candymaker
23 State firmly
24 Bruce of Dr. Watson fame
25 Hoop
28 Capitol Hill gang
31 Hapless hare hunter
32 Puts up curtains
33 Dr. Dolittle's dog
34 On ___ with (equal)
35 Timothy Dalton's homeland
36 Links warning
37 Blue Jackets' org.
38 Rx supply
39 "Suzanne" songwriter Leonard
40 Packet near a soup bowl
42 January birthstone
43 1992 Joe Pesci title role
44 *Bonanza* brother
45 Taiwan capital
47 Disney film
51 Fab Four film
52 "The Tennessee Waltz" composer
54 Colleague of Agatha and Dashiell
55 Café client
56 Osprey's cousin
57 Richard in *The Invisible Boy*
58 Alums
59 Loch ___ Monster

DOWN

1 Love's antithesis
2 "Beauty ___ the eye ... "
3 *Dennis the Menace* girl
4 Knockout punch
5 Bordeaux, e.g.
6 Grease pencil
7 Start of a tot's chant
8 Popular bread
9 Salary
10 Tool for fixing a slip
11 Merry Men member
12 Musket ammo
13 "You can't pray ___"
18 "The White Cliffs of ___"
22 Future turtles
24 Fifth canonical hour
25 Not worth a hill of ___

26 Highest wolf pack rank
27 Lana Lang's hometown
28 Rings up
29 "Yes ___ Bob!"
30 Drained
32 *Roots* author
35 Manitoba capital
36 Deserted
38 Christmas tree
39 Hindu social system
41 Appreciative diner
42 They have no chance
44 Hemmed and ___
45 Quaker pronoun
46 Wispy
47 Greek cheese
48 Royal address
49 London's ___ of Court
50 Birthday topics
53 Q-tip target

★ BrainSnack®—Red Letter

Which letter still needs to be colored red?

CONNECT TWO

An oxymoron is a combination of seemingly contradictory or incongruous words, such as "science fiction"(science means "knowledge or study dealing with facts or truth" while fiction means "an imagined or invented creation"). Connect the words with meanings that oppose each other and make oxymorons.

BAD	ODDS
CIVIL	BOAT
EVEN	LUCK
HOUSE	DISOBEDIENCE

★ Electro Technology

All the words are hidden vertically, horizontal or diagonally—in both directions. The letters that remain unused form a sentence from left to right.

```
A N N G N I N T H G I L E L E
L E O C T R I C A C E L R A N
M E R D N G I N E C T O E M G
O R T Y R C A N N R T I O P I
D O C N E F E A R C R D W T N
U T E A O R D E U O E E S S E
L A L M O E B D T M V U S R E
A L E O P A N S C A E S A U R
T O N M T O I D W T H E O R F
I S I T C S X O B H C T I W S
O I E I N I R A D I O T U B E
N R M A E C S F P E R V O L T
Y E R B I O M M H E A A T H E
S T U M E M A T Y I R R C S D
A L Z T R E H N S D P E T H O
B I I N D U C T I O N Y P H N
S F R E Q U E N C Y I C S M A
Y T I C A P A C S E S I O N A
```

DYNAMO
EARTH
ELECTRON
ENGINEER
FILTER
FREQUENCY
FUSE
HERTZ
IMPEDANCE
INDUCTION
ISOLATOR
LAMP
LIGHTNING
MICROWAVE
MODEM
MODULATION
NOISE
PHYSICS
RADIO TUBE
SEMICONDUCTOR
SWITCH
SWITCH BOX
TRANSISTOR
VOLT

AMPERE	BATTERY	CAPACITY
ANODE	BULB	CONDUCTOR

WORD SHRINKS

Make each word shorter by taking away one letter at a time but keeping the remaining letters in their original order and form a new word. Do this as many times as possible, forming a new word as each letter is deleted. Example : PLATE ➡ LATE ➡ ATE ➡ AT

STAND

★★ Open Winners (Tennis) by Karen Peterson

ACROSS

1 "Beat it!"
5 Book keeper?
10 Took off on
14 Word form for "air"
15 *Pagliacci* baritone role
16 Dover fish
17 Cambodian coin
18 Not so new
19 *The Sixth Sense* boy
20 Guinness superlative
22 See 30 Down
24 Post-OR destination
25 Strictly forbid
26 "My Way" singer
30 2003 U.S. Open winner
34 "The Cradle of Texas Liberty"
35 Frames of mind
37 Rob Roy's negative
38 One of TV's Cartwrights
39 Scope
40 Caroline Wozniacki, for one
41 ___ jam (stuck)
42 *Pippin* choreographer
43 Islamic lamp spirit
44 Light rock songs
46 Fish that attach
48 Suffer ill health
49 Canned ham brand
50 2002 U.S. Open winner
54 Talked into
58 "___ You Babe": Sonny & Cher
59 Adder secretion
61 Mark a ballot
62 Decor change
63 *Germinal* novelist Zola
64 Not left out of
65 Leak slowly
66 Subleases
67 Lincoln's coin

DOWN

1 Starr or Simpson
2 Darth Vader's daughter
3 City S of Moscow
4 2008 U.S. Open winner
5 2011 U.S. Open winner
6 News anchor Lester
7 Conclude
8 Willingly, once
9 Portend
10 Scale
11 On one's uppers
12 Model Macpherson
13 Fall game?
21 Prefix meaning "outside"
23 Pappies
26 Bengali "master"
27 *Silver Shark* novelist Andrews
28 Stuffy-sounding
29 Run up
30 2006 U.S. Open winner (with 22-A)
31 "The bombs bursting ___ ...": Key
32 Showy plant
33 Wails for the dead
36 Switch "ups"
39 1969 U.S. Open winner
40 2011 U.S. Open winner
42 "Vanity ___": Thackeray
43 Key of a Pachelbel canon: Abbr.
45 Item stolen at airports
47 "Rag Mop" quartet member
50 Old letter opener
51 *A Death in the Family* novelist
52 Fashion
53 Star-dotted
54 Quarterback McCoy
55 Unattached
56 Lord Wimsey's alma mater
57 Fender bender reminder
60 *Little Birds* author Anaïs

★★ Number Cluster

Complete the grid by constituting adjoining clusters that consist of as many cubes as the number on the cubes. At cube 5, for instance, you will have to make a five-cube cluster. Two or more figure cubes of the same value belong to the same cluster. You can only place your cubes along horizontal and/or vertical lines.

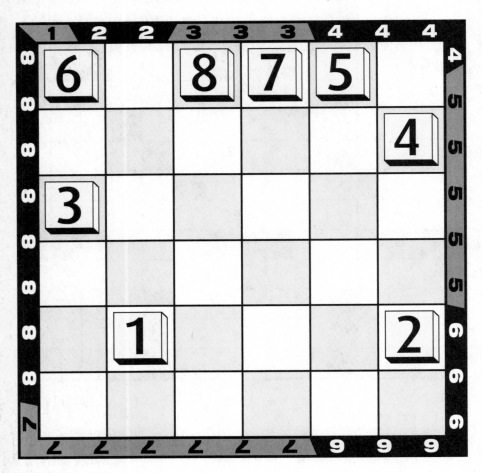

DOUBLETALK

Homophones are words that share the same pronunciation, no matter how they are spelled. If they are spelled differently then they are called heterographs. Find heterographs meaning:

A SEAT FOR A KING and TOSSED

★★★ BrainSnack®—City Break

Which city (1–6) is not written like the other 5 cities?

AMSTEЯDAM 1
BЯUXE⅃⅃ƎS 2
CHIƆAƍO 3
KAAꟼƧTAD 4
PARIS 5
ЯƎYꓘ⅃AVÌK 6

FRIENDS?

What do the following words have in common?

PRIEST NATION MAN FATHER SISTER

★★ Open Winners (Golf) by Karen Peterson

ACROSS

1 Long-necked pear
5 Poison ivy's family
10 Jack Frost's canvas, at times
14 Asian nurse
15 Planet for a canine?
16 One of Athena's names
17 Hayworth in *Pal Joey*
18 Mumble's friend in *Happy Feet*
19 Where to find anvils
20 Star-studded
22 2011 U.S. Open winner
24 Dame Edna, for one
25 Pipe fitter's joint
26 U2 guitarist
30 2010 U.S. Women's Open winner
34 Cause of wrinkles
35 Conductor Zubin
37 Tokyo of old
38 "As ___ saying"
39 Greeting for Dolly
40 "Grace Before Meat" essayist
41 Upstate NY campus
42 *Pagliacci* fool
43 Guitar ridges
44 1997 British Open winner
46 Heartfelt
48 Sheena Easton, née ___
49 Six, to Pavarotti
50 Kindle Fire operating system
54 1994 U.S. Women's Open winner
58 Smile
59 *Cinderella* dog
61 House overhang
62 Architectural pier
63 Hologram maker
64 China neighbor
65 Connery in *The Rock*
66 Dais VIP
67 Nine-digit IDs

DOWN

1 Happy hour stops
2 Neglect to mention
3 Satisfy totally
4 2011 Australian Open winner
5 Moved suddenly
6 Suffix with cell
7 Unspeaking
8 It's split at CERN
9 Orchestral work
10 Spanish rice dish
11 Banned orchard treatment
12 Franco in *Camelot*
13 "Careful now"
21 ___ Macbeth
23 Intestinal parts
26 Rotate rapidly
27 Mandel or Long
28 "The Lovely" Muse

29 Polish
30 Paris fashion house
31 Shoving match escalation
32 Changes one's story
33 Rake over the coals
36 Wallach or Whitney
39 Ghastly
40 1997 U.S. Open winner
42 South Seas starch
43 Gratis
45 1986 British Open winner
47 On leave, maybe
50 "___ Ben Adhem": Ogden Nash
51 Hawaiian honker
52 Contents of some bases
53 A little liquor

54 Ko-Ko's dagger
55 1981 B.C. Open winner
56 River to the Severn
57 Loch 23 miles long
60 2008 Rose Bowl winners

★★★ Sport Maze

Draw the shortest way from the ball to the goal. You can only move along vertical and horizontal lines, not along diagonal lines. The figure on each square indicates the number of squares the ball must be moved in the same direction. You can change direction at each stop.

2	4	1	3	5	5
5	3	3	3	2	5
4	3	1	3	2	
5	2	1	0	1	4
1	3	2	4	2	3
4	2	4	3	3	3

LETTER LINE

Put a letter in each of the squares below to make a word which means "HANGING FRUIT." These numbered clues refer to other words which can be made from the whole.

6 4 3 2 7 8 1 TRADES; 6 8 7 5 1 INFUSES;
1 2 4 3 3 10 GLITTERY; 1 2 3 4 5 NOT BRICKS; 5 7 4 9 1 PUTS ON

1	2	3	4	5	6	7	8	9	10

★ Word Sudoku

Complete the grid so that each row, each column and each 3 x 3 frame contains the nine letters from the black box below. The hidden nine-letter word is in the diagonal from top left to bottom right.

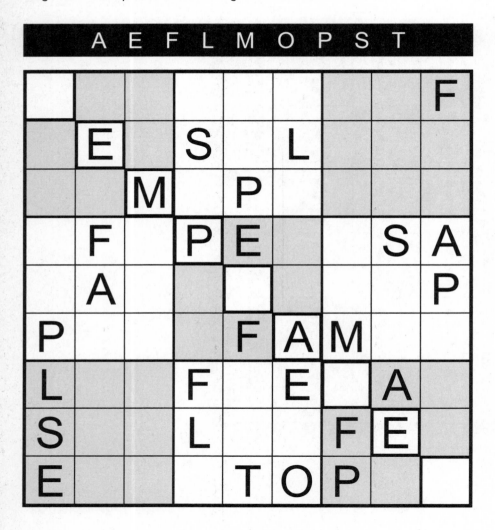

A E F L M O P S T

BLOCK ANAGRAM

Form the words that are described in the brackets with the letters above the grid. An extra letter is already in the right place.

TART ALARM (weaponless self-defense)

☐ ☐ ☐ ☐ I ☐ ☐　☐ ☐ ☐

★★ Best Supporting Actors by John McCarthy

ACROSS

1 Suvari in "American Beauty"
5 Unaccompanied
10 To ___ (precisely)
14 Military absentee
15 Suppress news
16 Caplet
17 *Sayonara* Oscar winner
19 Islamic prayer leader
20 ___ comforts
21 Artichoke morsels
23 Summon to court
24 Heavenly prefix
25 Work one's wiles upon
28 Sale caveat
29 Undergrad degrees
32 Chicago hub
33 To the point, ironically
34 "Be Prepared" org.
35 Defensive spray
36 Julianne in *The Hours*
37 Goalie's glove
38 Rub the wrong way
39 Checkroom error
40 Painter Matisse
41 Roman 450
42 Like pawn-shop items
43 Ted of *CSI*
44 Emends
46 New York paper
47 iPhone feature
49 Drapes
53 Represent in drawing
54 *A Streetcar Named Desire* Oscar winner
56 Schoenberg's *Moses und ___*
57 Tape over a video
58 Darth Vader's daughter
59 Prevent from scoring
60 Fencing blade
61 Shrill cry

DOWN

1 Anthony in *El Cantante*
2 Washstand pitcher
3 Brood of pheasants
4 Canned tuna
5 Shrewd
6 British bottle size
7 Plains tribesman
8 Persona ___ grata
9 Preserve as sacred
10 Beelike
11 *Mystic River* Oscar winner
12 Israeli port
13 Spreading trees
18 Not merely decorative
22 "... ___, and Juliet is the sun!"
24 Take illegally
25 Funny
26 Drive ___ bargain
27 *Mister Roberts* Oscar winner
28 Not whispered
30 Houston slugger
31 Tuxedo trim
33 Cartons
36 Goofs
37 In the mind
39 *The Ghost and Mrs. ___* (1947)
40 ___ *luego!*
43 Upstairs window
45 Crane on *Boston Legal*
46 Public sentiment
47 Decent
48 Leeds river
49 Zodiac crustacean
50 ___ fixe
51 Goldman on *Family Guy*
52 Ginger cookie
55 Coach Parseghian

★★★ Sudoku

Fill in the grid so that each row, each column and each 3 x 3 frame contains
every number from 1 to 9.

						2		6
	8						3	
	7			6	2		5	
	1				4			
8				2				
	3		6				8	2
			4	1	7	9		8
	6	7	2		5			1
1			3				2	

SANDWICH

What five-letter word belongs between the word on the left and the word on the right, so that
the first and second word, and the second and third word, each form a common compound word
or phrase?

STAGE _ _ _ _ _ LINE

★★★ BrainSnack®—Missing Cube

Which cube is missing from the last set?

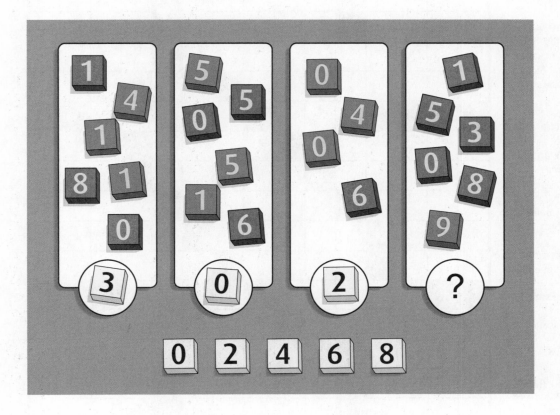

CHANGE ONE, CHANGE ANOTHER

Change one letter in the first word to create a second word, then change one letter in the second word to create a third word which will become the final word by changing one letter. There may be more than one possible answer.

SONG ➡ _ _ _ _ ➡ _ _ _ _ ➡ TOES

★★ Best Supporting Actresses by John McCarthy

ACROSS

1 Stay ___ even keel
5 Brown ermine
10 Over and done with
14 Official records
15 Unfamiliar language
16 City of central Sicily
17 *Paper Moon* Oscar winner
19 Use the shears
20 Charcuterie offerings
21 Heirs split it
23 Gabor and Perón
24 Fresh and firm
25 Stay
28 Gather up
29 Quick Murray point
32 *Waiting for Lefty* playwright
33 Emotional shocks
34 Geometry proof ender
35 Stratagem
36 Comedienne Essman
37 Crooned
38 What makes a chef chief?
39 Narrow groove
40 Job reward
41 *Hey Jude* refrain words
42 Presley's middle name
43 Put on
44 Cut off
46 Government center
47 Like Rapunzel's hair
49 Most inane
53 Leslie Caron musical
54 *The Accidental Tourist* Oscar winner
56 Mid-month, in old Rome
57 Morgan of *30 Rock*
58 "Monster" lizard
59 Bender
60 Boggs and Irwin
61 Swan genus

DOWN

1 Mare's meal
2 Scholastic sports org.
3 Outermost Aleutian island
4 Disgust
5 Adman's creation
6 Pitchfork parts
7 Binary-code digits
8 Palindromic title
9 Put up with
10 Nuisances
11 *The Piano* Oscar winner
12 Bad mood
13 Storage medium
18 Mrs. Jay Leno
22 Drinks politely
24 Salsa legend Cruz
25 Atkinson in *Bean*
26 Patsy's *Ab Fab* friend
27 *The Fighter* Oscar winner
28 Pitcher's aid
30 Use a thurible
31 Made a border
33 He sits in judgment
36 Intensity
37 Capital of Chile
39 Prepare for retirement
40 Willy Wonka's creator Dahl
43 Late flights
45 Just get by
46 Subsequently
47 Flutter
48 Venetian beach resort
49 Big-top barker
50 The forces of darkness
51 Bucolic structure
52 Romanov ruler
55 Big Band ___

★ Spot the Differences

Find the nine differences in the image on the right.

END GAME

The words you are seeking all have the letters END in them in the position indicated. When you have found all of the answers, from the clues on the right, one column will reveal the END GAME word which help you to listen.

E N D _ _ _ _		Equipped with a quality
E N D _ _ _ _		A tactical move
_ E N D _ _ _		Car protecters
_ E N D _ _ _ _		Upright

★ Horoscope

Fill in the grid so that every row, every column and every frame of six boxes contains six different symbols: health, work, money, happiness, family and love. Look at the row or column that corresponds with your sign of the zodiac and find out which of the six symbols are important for you today. The symbols appear in increasing order of importance (1–6). It's up to you to translate the meaning of each symbol to your specific situation.

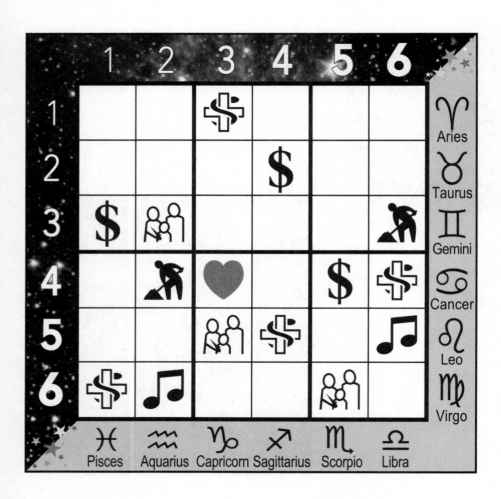

REPOSITION PREPOSITION

Unscramble HOTTER WEIGHT and find a double-word preposition.

★★ Futoshiki

Fill in the 5 x 5 grid with the numbers from 1 to 5 once per row and column, while following the greater than/lesser than symbols shown. There is only one valid solution that can be reached through logic and clear thinking alone!

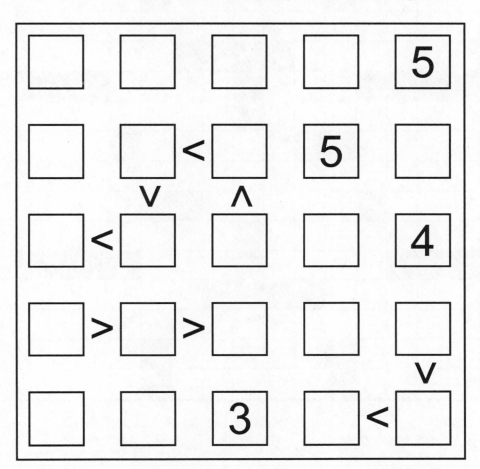

LETTERBLOCKS

Move the letterblocks around so that words are formed on top and below that you can associate with biology. In one block, the letter from the top row has been switched with the letter from the bottom row.

★★★ Famous Arians by Kelly Lynch

ACROSS

1 *The Good Earth* wife
5 Silicon Valley giant
10 Gothic arch
14 Big wheels for a big wheel
15 Weighted net
16 Bring up baby
17 Arian Renaissance man
20 *Terms of Endearment* heroine
21 Forgetfulness
22 *The Chill* detective Archer
24 Getz of jazz
26 Filled-pasta dish
30 Males with mail
34 Fail to name
35 Lopez in *The Dirty Dozen*
37 ABBA drummer Brunkert
38 Arian pontiff
42 Poetic for "before"
43 "Set Fire to the Rain" singer
44 Cambodian currency
45 Twine threads
47 Narrow swords
50 Fish with "wings"
51 "Seats sold out" sign
52 Hold back, as a story
55 USO show audience
60 Arian U.S. President
65 Dalai ___
66 Canton capital west of Zurich
67 On the Adriatic
68 *Shih Ching* verses
69 Get bent out of shape
70 Genie's home

DOWN

1 Pueblo cooking vessel
2 In ___ of (supplanting)
3 Companion of Venus
4 Taboo
5 Where shekels are spent
6 *Our Idiot Brother* brother
7 Padre's brother
8 Tom Brady's target
9 Grassy tract
10 Help get settled
11 Refined chap
12 Per capita
13 "Clinton's Folly" canal
18 He sang about Alice
19 Pickle brand
23 Testifier
24 Web designers?
25 Collette of *United States of Tara*
26 It's good to know them
27 Lifeless
28 Puff adder, e.g.
29 Suffix for London
31 Nerve, in slang
32 Tiny eel
33 Exemplar of toughness
36 Diminutive noun suffix
39 Smoothie fruit
40 Swirling water
41 Corn or angle starter
46 Kitchen emanations
48 Tricky
49 Skin orifice
52 City SE of Cherbourg
53 "___ no idea!"
54 "Bring It on Home ___": Cooke
56 Like courtroom testimony
57 Pelion's sister peak
58 "A ___ lovely as a tree": Kilmer
59 Crackle's colleague
61 Droop
62 Cyclist Ullrich
63 Roy Halladay stat
64 Out there

★ Antiques

All the words are hidden vertically, horizontally or diagonally—in both directions. The letters that remain unused form a sentence from left to right.

```
M W A T C H O R W E Z N O R B
E S H E L V E S C O R I G I N
R E E R A R C E L N O T W U C
O R K C C U P B O A R D S K R
M S U H C H E T C H I N G S Y
I L A E S J U H K G E N D E S
R A S S E P A C S N W O T D T
R N T T I I L D S I L V E R A
O O A N R T A P E S T R Y D L
R I W S C A S L I S N E T U R
T T A D E O I C O I I G O L D
S I S A L T T S O C O G N S T
S D H I X D E T R E D T N E E
O A S E L A I N O L O C E L N
S R T C L O T H I N G B L B I
I T A L A I D N U S E A Y A B
L E N G R A V I N G S N T T A
K T D I Q U P A T I N A S E C
```

COLONIAL
COTTON
CRYSTAL
CUPBOARDS
DESIGN
DESK
ENGRAVINGS
ETCHINGS
GOLD
MIRROR
ORIGIN
PATINA
RARE
RUG
SHELVES
SILK
SILVER
STYLE
SUNDIAL
TABLES
TAPESTRY
TEXTILE
TOWNSCAPES
TRADITIONAL
UTENSILS
WASHSTAND
WATCH
WOOD

BRONZE
CABINET

CHAIRS
CHEST

CLOCK
CLOTHING

DOUBLETALK

Homophones are words that share the same pronunciation, no matter how they are spelled. If they are spelled differently then they are called heterographs. Find heterographs meaning:

A SPACE BETWEEN ROWS and SURROUNDED BY WATER

★★ Sunny Weather

Where will the sun shine? With the knowledge that each arrow points to a place where a symbol should be, can you locate the sunny spots? The symbols cannot be next to each other vertically, horizontally or diagonally. A symbol cannot be placed on top of an arrow. We show one symbol.

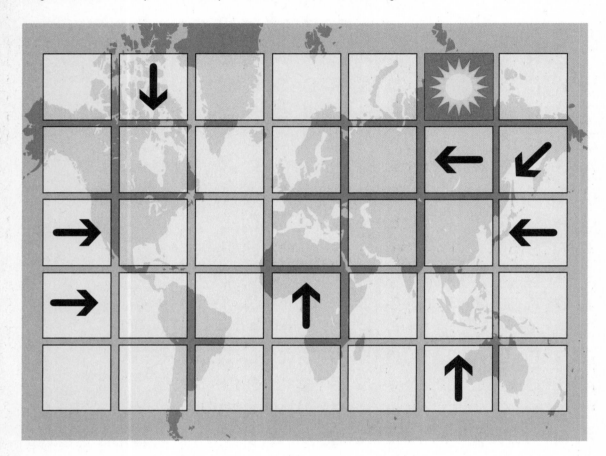

ONE LETTER LESS OR MORE

The word on the right side contains the letters of the word on the left side plus or minus the letter in the middle. One letter is already in the right place.

C A N C E L E D -C □ □ □ A □ □ □

★★★ Famous Leos by Kelly Lynch

ACROSS

1 Sellouts
5 Twig broom
10 Upscale cameras
14 Pronto, initially
15 Bogart's *High Sierra* role
16 Drudgery
17 Leo actor
20 *The Stepford Wives* protagonist
21 Tested, as a load
22 Biol. and geol.: Abbr.
24 Golden Calf deity
25 African adventure series (1966–69)
28 Tempers
32 Olympic swords
33 "Big ___" (David Ortiz)
35 Month before *juin*
36 Leo film director
40 Wahine's wreath
41 Rice-A-___
42 Soil
43 1935 Masters winner Gene
46 Bose products
48 Pulls a fast one
49 Ankles
50 Criticism
53 African grasslands
57 Leo NBA great
61 In a line
62 Mystery Writers of America award
63 Prefix for bus
64 "Take ___ your leader"
65 Fiend
66 Like Felix Unger

DOWN

1 Muslim pilgrimage
2 Golfer Aoki
3 Blue Nile source
4 Old maid
5 Ritzy part of L.A.
6 Piercing site
7 Mex. lady
8 *No Country for ___ Men* (2007)
9 Wrench user
10 Quash
11 SoHo apartment
12 Abundantly prevalent
13 Flexible Flyer
18 Box eggs
19 Rangy
23 Suction devices
24 Protestant denomination
25 Super buys
26 Cop ___ (beg for leniency)
27 Fermented milk drink
29 Con ___ (lovingly, in music)
30 Milk prefix
31 Turbaned Punjabis
34 Rhone tributary
37 Caught in a cloudburst
38 Ward ___ (local politico)
39 Church music maker
44 Intermission follower
45 Suffix with paleo-
47 Place to order a round
50 Competed in 500 freestyle
51 Spare item
52 Loads
54 Diana Rigg's title
55 Cohen-Chang on *Glee*
56 Uptight state
58 Citrus beverage
59 *Grand Hotel* studio
60 Vietnamese emperor ___ Dai

★★★ BrainSnack®—Current Account

Which four digits complete the account number on the fourth card?

CONNECT TWO

An oxymoron is a combination of seemingly contradictory or incongruous words, such as "science fiction"(science means "knowledge or study dealing with facts or truth" while fiction means "an imagined or invented creation"). Connect the words with meanings that oppose each other and make oxymorons.

HALF	HEALTH
INVISIBLE	FULL
ILL	BOY
OLD	INK

★★★ Kakuro

Each number in a black area is the sum of the numbers that you have to enter in the next empty boxes beside or below. The empty boxes that make up the sum are called a run. The sum of the across run is written above the diagonal in the black area and the sum of the down run is written below the diagonal. Runs can only contain the numbers 1 through 9 and each number in a run can only be used once. The gray boxes contain only odd numbers and the white only even numbers.

UNCANNY TURN

Rearrange the letters of the phrase below to form a cognate anagram, one which is related or connected in meaning to the original phrase. The answer can be one or more words.

TURN TO CRY HOME

★★★ Famous Sagittarians by Kelly Lynch

ACROSS

1 Ibuprofen target
5 Cleveland's Gund
10 Bones of *Sleepy Hollow*
14 Made some beds
15 German engraver
16 Eisenhower, to MacArthur
17 Sagittarian actor
20 Handbook
21 Willows for weavers
22 November 11 honoree
24 Son of Ares
25 Georgia's capital
29 Morty and Ferdie, to Mickey
33 Engine conduit
34 Peninsula near Hong Kong
36 Third of XXI
37 Sagittarian novelist
41 Undershirt
42 Sniffers
43 Sacramento arena
44 Bride of Dionysus
46 Fertilized eggs
49 Burns out
50 Up for payment
51 Signs of indifference
54 Chinese meditative exercises
59 Sagittarian painter
63 Death notice
64 Flout the rules
65 Beak part
66 Lily who sang soprano
67 As a result
68 Take notice

DOWN

1 "Excuse me ..."
2 Ballet conclusion
3 Chopped down
4 Jacob's hairy brother
5 Confuses
6 Scatter ___
7 Walk in a run
8 Classic beginning
9 Tree-dwelling
10 Expel
11 Bailiff's command
12 Sulfur attribute
13 Clothing store section
18 Norah Jones' father
19 14-legged crustacean
23 L.A. and London dailies
24 Like Tiffany displays
25 Eighth Greek letter
26 Hole-making bug
27 Japanese immigrant
28 Albanian coin
30 "___ inch a king!": Shak.
31 Word after "roger"
32 Grain holders
35 Big name in bandages
38 Deep blue
39 Peerless
40 No-brainer card game
45 18-and-over crowd
47 Change in form
48 Bridges in *Norma Rae*
51 "Freeze!"
52 Emmett Kelly role
53 Once-great city, perhaps
55 Chickenpox symptom
56 Canadian tribe
57 Companion of now
58 Secured
60 Pronoun for a plane
61 Dark time, to a bard
62 Varnish substance

★★ Word Sudoku

Complete the grid so that each row, each column and each 3 x 3 frame contains the nine letters from the black box below. The hidden nine-letter word is in the diagonal from top left to bottom right.

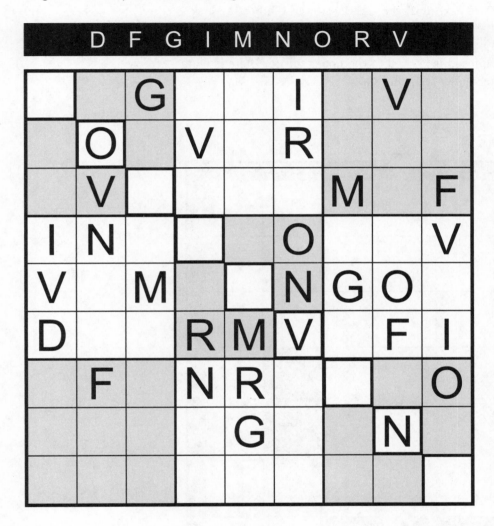

SANDWICH

What four-letter word belongs between the word on the left and the word on the right, so that the first and second word, and the second and third word, each form a common compound word or phrase?

THUNDER _ _ _ _ GOWN

★★ Keep Going

Start on a blank square of your choice and connect as many blank squares as possible with one single continuous line. You can only connect squares along vertical and horizontal lines, not along diagonal lines. You must continue the connecting line up until the next obstacle, i.e., the rim of the box, a black square or a square that has already been used. You can change direction at any obstacle you meet. Each square can be used only once. The number of blank squares that will be left unused is marked in the upper square. There is more than one solution. We show only one solution.

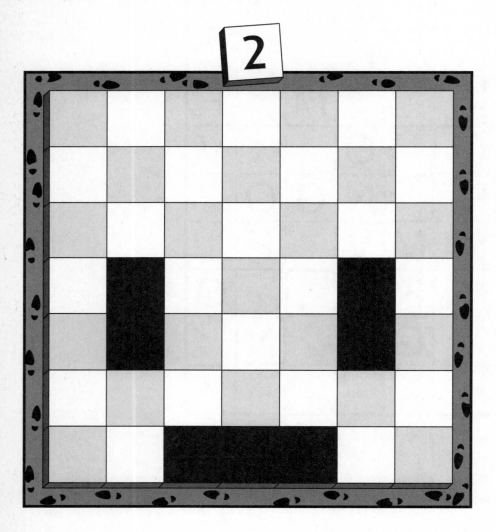

REPOSITION PREPOSITION

Unscramble NARCOTIC GOD and find a two-word preposition.

★★★ Tee for Two by Cindy Wheeler

ACROSS

1 Falling-out
5 Mold or fashion
10 All-purpose trucks
14 Matty who hit .342 in 1966
15 DNA shape
16 Showering state
17 Money of Yemen
18 Put in office
19 Marathoner Zátopek
20 Yarn
22 Pottery glaze
24 Kennel guest
25 Optimistic
26 Lawyer's case
30 Stroller occupant
33 Poppin' Fresh is this
34 It calls for a blessing
36 Krupp of the NHL
37 Additional
38 Sweet ____ College
39 Rob Reiner's alma mater
40 Sign a contract
41 Disney film set in China
42 Cross-examiner, e.g.
43 Links reservation
45 General pardon
47 Shaggy Tibetans
48 Financial assistance
49 Half a rack
51 Beat a hasty retreat
56 Pressing
57 Suffix with fraud
59 Ballerina Spessivtzeva
60 Soon enough
61 Like a flophouse
62 Godsend
63 Groening or Dillon
64 Medal of ____
65 "Pushover" singer James

DOWN

1 Mouth-puckering
2 Skating star Kulik
3 Stud farm arrival
4 Newspaper ad type
5 Scabbard
6 Dante's inferno
7 Opposite the wind
8 Movie, slangily
9 Outside
10 Nervous
11 Flatteners of spare tires
12 Falco in *The Sopranos*
13 Liquidate
21 NASDAQ sector
23 A don't
26 Be a doorman
27 Hundred ____ (long odds)
28 Ragtime dance
29 NFL Hall-of-Famer Neale
30 "... faster ____ speeding bullet"
31 Baby who doesn't sleep at night?
32 About to cry
35 Leon Panetta's org.
38 Bouncer specialty
39 Was
41 Masters winner Weir
42 Has ____ (knows somebody)
44 Aptitude
46 Saint Stephen, e.g.
49 Man not born of woman
50 *Black Swan* heroine
51 *Not Another ____ Movie* (2001)
52 Nullify
53 Rafts
54 "____ the Sun in the Morning"
55 Turner in *Peyton Place*
58 Durocher of baseball

The grid is a 15×15 crossword puzzle with numbered cells at positions 1–65.

★★★ Sport Maze

Draw the shortest way from the ball to the goal. You can only move along vertical and horizontal lines, not along diagonal lines. The figure on each square indicates the number of squares the ball must be moved in the same direction. You can change direction at each stop.

3	2	5	5	3	1
4	1	2	2	4	1
4	4	2	2	4	5
2	0	1	3	1	1
4	1	4	4	2	4
4		5	3	1	3

LETTERBLOCKS

Move the letterblocks around so that words are formed on top and below that you can associate with basketball.

D F R A R W O
D R N U B O E

★★★ Sudoku

Fill in the grid so that each row, each column and each 3 x 3 frame contains every number from 1 to 9.

1			8					
4							5	
			9	6		7		
			3					
	9				6			7
		7				8	2	3
	8			9		5		
2	6	3				4	1	9

DOODLE PUZZLE

A doodle puzzle is a combination of images, letters and/or numbers that represent a word or a concept. If you cannot solve a doodle puzzle, do not look at the answer right away. Think hard—and outside the box.

E

★★★ BrainSnack®—Game On

The image on the screen of which video game machine is incorrect?

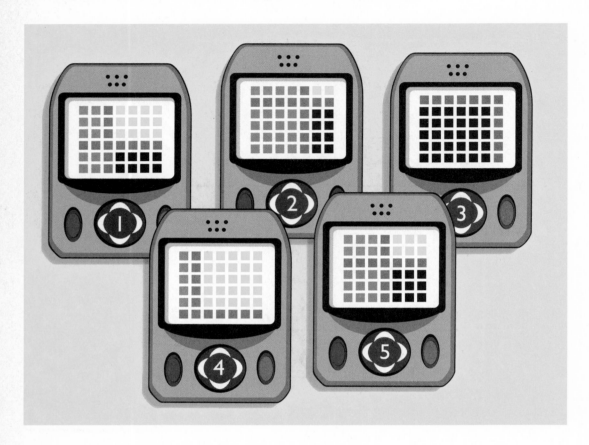

BLOCK ANAGRAM

Form the words that are described in the brackets with the letters above the grid. Extra letters are already in the right place.

BORING SWAN (sliding down a snow-covered slope)

		O						D			

★★★ Themeless by John M. Samson

ACROSS

1 *The ___ of March* (2011)
5 Buddhist shrine
10 Annoys
14 Boston cager, for short
15 Vietnamese capital
16 Fender flaw
17 Budgie is a little one
19 Brainchild
20 Handel opus
21 Befitting
23 White knight
24 Candied, in cookery
25 *48 ___* (Nick Nolte film)
26 Tasmanian duckbill
29 Diamond feature
32 Bearings
33 Palm smartphone
34 "Just my luck!"
35 Pasta pick
36 Dispatched
37 "Hi-De-Ho Man" Calloway
38 Frankenstein, for one
39 Too severe
40 Broadcast
42 Prohibit
43 Did an axel
44 Focus of LAX screenings
48 Make waves
50 Plundered
51 Meter man?
52 "Blue" singer
54 Bugbear
55 Say "li'l," say
56 What a stitch in time saves
57 Yosemite Sam, for one
58 Yellow weed
59 And others

DOWN

1 Blood of the gods
2 "John ___ Tractor": Judds
3 Greek name for Greece
4 Baseball features
5 Coasts
6 Malayan mammal
7 "Golden Rule" word
8 "Annabel Lee" poet
9 Boeing product
10 Dumbness
11 Cayenne flakes
12 ___-jerk reaction
13 Hexagram
18 Place for a net
22 Charlie Brown's cry
24 Close in *Albert Nobbs*
26 Burgundy grape
27 Footed vases
28 Clockmaker Thomas
29 Truism
30 Winglike
31 Southwestern horseman
32 Be worthy of
35 Booklet
36 Cheerfully optimistic
38 Ag degrees
39 Viking of comics
41 Spruce up
42 Fife or Frank
44 Rings
45 Come clean about
46 Davis in *Tootsie*
47 Ford of dubious fame
48 Catch sight of
49 Cartoon possum
50 Open ocean
53 She, in Lisbon

★ New York

All the words are hidden vertically, horizontally or diagonally—in both directions. The letters that remain unused form a sentence from left to right.

```
S E E K N A Y N I R I S H J O
B L O O M B E R G E H W Y A R
O R O O S E V E L T A R K Z I
I S P H Y A W D A O R B O Z N
M T E R A B A C T E L T M M E
O T R H S E H C I N E M A U D
H C A P O N E E N A M D R S Q
U K B U A R A T O E R S A I O
D N R F N C H I N E S E T C T
S I O H A I R P L A N E H E U
O C O N I T W P E A D C O N A
N K K T I B P H O N T S N W I
T S L T R A H T S U H I I E F
L E Y O G A P P D R I N C G F
L A N I G S O B A S E B A L L
F X B N S N E E U Q I G P T S
M I N A I L U I G E M M E T S
B E R N A S D A Q S T A T E S
```

BROOKLYN
CABARET
CAPONE
CHINESE
CINEMA
DE NIRO
DUTCH
GERSHWIN
GIULIANI
HARLEM
HUDSON
IRISH
ITALIANS
JAZZ MUSIC
KNICKS
LATINO
MARATHON
METS
NASDAQ
OPERA
PACINO
QUEENS
ROOSEVELT
TENNIS
YANKEES

AIRPLANE   BIG APPLE   BROADWAY
BASEBALL   BLOOMBERG   BRONX

DOUBLETALK

Homophones are words that share the same pronunciation, no matter how they are spelled. If they are spelled differently then they are called heterographs. Find heterographs meaning:

A SIGH OF DESPAIR and BIGGER

★★★ BrainSnack®—Switch Around

Which switch (1–4) should replace the question mark?

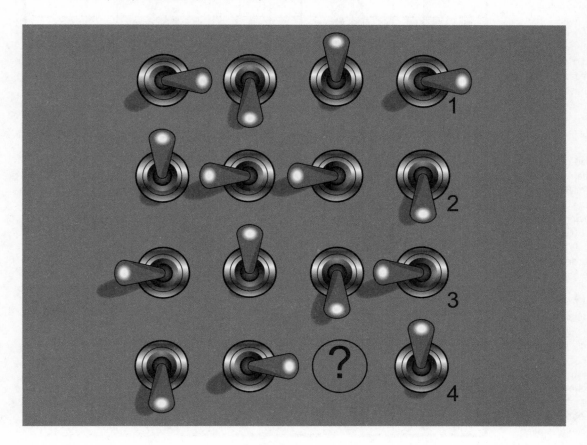

ONE LETTER LESS OR MORE

The word on the right side contains the letters of the word on the left side plus or minus the letter in the middle. One letter is already in the right place.

| C | A | N | N | A | B | I | S | +L | | | | N | | | | | |

★★★ Eastwood Films by Cindy Wheeler

ACROSS

1 Filter through
5 Out of place
10 Hebrew month
14 West End opener
15 Extend a note
16 River near the Red Sea
17 "I confess that I have no desire to confess." film
19 Fumble
20 Defers
21 Austrian cakes
23 Canadian loonies
24 Cyrus of *Hannah Montana*
25 Increasingly sore
28 To an extent
31 Research funds
32 Squad car sound
33 Rosary bead
34 Isn't misused?
35 Joined forces
36 Hebrides hill
37 *Family Guy* daughter
38 Susann's *Valley of the ___*
39 Yellow finch
40 Good enough
42 How acrobats perform
43 Childhood illness
44 "Love Song" singer Bareilles
45 Mumbai masters
47 Mood
51 Viking war god
52 "I seen the angel of death, he's got snake eyes." film
54 Boxers and pugs
55 Sorghum
56 Call for
57 Silvery
58 Trample
59 Spaces between teeth

DOWN

1 Drops off
2 Beige
3 Greek vowels
4 Zero in on
5 Laundry employee
6 Dweebs
7 Black cuckoos
8 Pigsty
9 Double-crossed
10 Prince Harry's uncle
11 "I know what you're thinking, punk." film
12 Hydrocortisone additive
13 Sales folks
18 Palindromic principle
22 *Victory Square* novelist Steinhauer
24 Societal customs
25 Long-tailed lizard
26 Shed tears
27 "You don't remember me, do you?" film
28 Crabwalk
29 Be of help
30 Extremely small
32 River deposits
35 Lather
36 Scolding
38 Not too bright
39 Watercress piece
41 Tonsil disorder
42 Despot
44 Squall
45 Cutty Sark cutter
46 Commotions
47 Do of the '60s
48 Eye membrane
49 Not superficial
50 Tim Tebow targets
53 Head case

★ Sudoku X

Fill in the grid so that each row, each column and each 3 x 3 frame contains every number from 1 to 9. The two main diagonals of the grid must also contain every number from 1 to 9.

						8		
	1		7		5			6
	8	7						
		4	6		1	5		7
	6	5	4	2				1
4				7	9		3	
	5		8	6			1	9
6					4	7	2	5

FRIENDS?

What do the following words have in common?

SCHOLAR WORKMAN CENSOR GUN READER

★★★ Binairo

Complete the grid with zeros and ones until there are 6 zeros and 6 ones in every row and every column. No more than two of the same number can be next to or under each other. Rows or columns with exactly the same content are not allowed. There is only one valid solution.

								O		
									O	
			O	O						O
										O
				I						
		I				I		O	O	
O			O							
	O				O	O				
							I	I		
O			O		O					
	O				O		O		O	
	O				I			O	O	

★★★ Vegan Special by Cindy Wheeler

ACROSS

1 Big Band music
6 Informal eatery
10 Mudpuppies
14 Norse pantheon
15 Libra birthstone
16 Bound to happen
17 Dense fogs
19 "Remembrance of a Garden" artist
20 Sugar suffix
21 One of the Munsters
23 Dinette set spot
27 Jimmy Eat World's music
28 Pride Lands female
30 Beatles song from *Let It Be*
34 Crimson-clad
35 *A Lesson From ___*: Fugard
37 Victoria's Secret purchase
38 Rowlands in *Hope Floats*
39 Fred and George Weasley, e.g.
40 Kind of ticket
41 "So there!"
42 Sleazy
43 Tropical vine
44 Reliable
46 Breastbone
48 Reggae precursor
49 1992 Wimbledon winner
50 Daytona Beach wear
54 Prefix for pod
55 Poland border river
56 *Toy Story* toy (with "Mr.")
62 Saucy
63 Spanker, for one
64 Present purpose
65 Drive by
66 Mideast cartel
67 Romance author Danielle

DOWN

1 Aphid's lunch
2 Petite
3 "Love ___ Simple Thing"
4 Grafton's ___ *for Noose*
5 Like LPs
6 Deal with
7 Simian
8 Work the land
9 Mexican model Benitez
10 Baffin Island native
11 Badly mistaken
12 It beats the deuce
13 Observed
18 Applications
22 Vintage vehicles
23 Ablaze
24 One-dimensional
25 U. of Nebraska team
26 Eligible for service
29 Worked in a lumber mill
30 *The Book of Mormon* awards
31 Basketball great Unseld
32 Oberon's planet
33 Cold-cuts choice
36 Hard cover
39 Undershirt
40 Sorvino in *Sweet Nothing*
42 *South Park* character
43 Scores
45 Mini and maxi
47 Sharp
50 Comet Hale-___
51 Conceit
52 ___ facto
53 Hotel freebie
54 Bathroom sprinkle
57 Musical link
58 Hard to keep in stock
59 Yale-to-Harvard direction
60 Pass with flying colors
61 Juan ___ Potro of tennis

★★ Keep Going

Start on a blank square of your choice and connect as many blank squares as possible with one single continuous line. You can only connect squares along vertical and horizontal lines, not along diagonal lines. You must continue the connecting line up until the next obstacle, i.e., the rim of the box, a black square or a square that has already been used. You can change direction at any obstacle you meet. Each square can be used only once. The number of blank squares that will be left unused is marked in the upper square. There is more than one solution. We show only one solution.

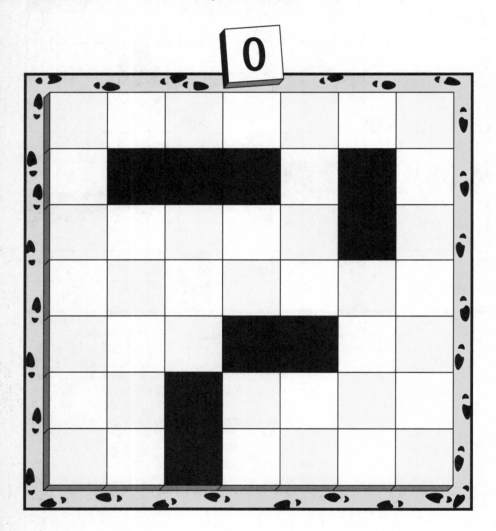

REPOSITION PREPOSITION

Unscramble RATTY CROON and find a two-word preposition.

★★★ BrainSnack®—Energy

Which 2 nuclei (1–3) have the same energy value knowing that nucleus A has just as much energy as nucleus B?

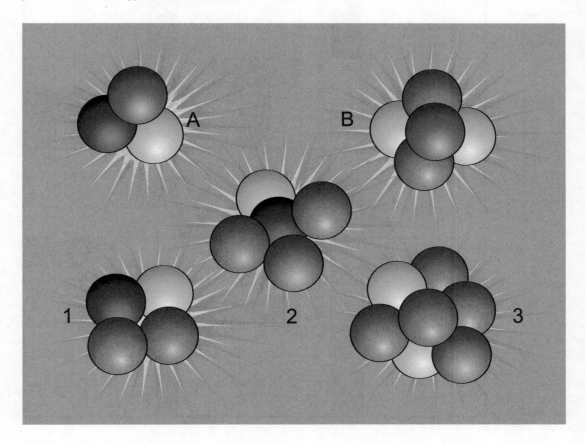

SANDWICH

What five-letter word belongs between the word on the left and the word on the right, so that the first and second word, and the second and third word, each form a common compound word or phrase?

SEARCH _ _ _ _ _ HOUSE

★★★ Name That Beatles Tune! by John M. Samson

ACROSS

1 Coffee cup holder
5 Yawning gulf
10 "Urgent!" on a memo
14 Narcissus spurned her
15 Tiki carver of New Zealand
16 Taboo
17 Commotion
18 Crack under pressure
19 In a frenzy
20 Mole passage
22 Moon of Saturn
24 Reverend famous for bloopers
26 Sired, Biblically
27 River of Poland
28 Lands
31 Publishing IDs
34 Inverts a stitch
36 It can be aroused
37 Give sparingly
38 Eeyore's creator
39 Mean mood
40 Memorable period
41 Piebald pony
42 Volcanic spillage
43 Capable of being cut
45 St. Paul's Cathedral designer
47 Odd fellows
48 "When I find myself in times of trouble ..." song
52 Empire State capital
54 *Prozac* ___ (2001)
55 Floral rings
56 "... I'm forever in your debt" song
60 Queen Elizabeth II's daughter
61 Piquant
62 Stood up
63 Pour
64 Bookie's figures
65 Brewing need
66 Circular current

DOWN

1 Orange scrapings
2 Throw a scene
3 *Ice Age* heavy
4 "The day breaks, your mind aches" song
5 More plentiful
6 Shearing noise
7 Word after hither
8 Indian term of respect
9 "These are words that go together well" song
10 Like old watches
11 "You know I believe and how" song
12 At a later time
13 Elbow in the ribs
21 Eagle catchers?
23 Sponsorship
25 Plunderings

26 Screeching bird
29 Light haircut
30 Arista
31 "Beware the ___ of March!"
32 Seeing red
33 "Take these broken wings ..." song
35 Last month: Abbr.
38 Earth's galaxy
39 Clean
41 Subatomic particle
42 Prefix for physics
44 "L'chaim" et al.
46 Milk curdler
49 Like pitchforks
50 Filleted
51 No friend
52 Female voice
53 Set the pace
57 Mined mineral

58 Extinct kiwi relative
59 Sancho's mount

★★★ Sport Maze

Draw the shortest way from the ball to the goal. You can only move along vertical and horizontal lines, not along diagonal lines. The figure on each square indicates the number of squares the ball must be moved in the same direction. You can change direction at each stop.

3	2	4	5	4	3
1	2	1	3	1	1
3	1	2	3	4	5
1	0	1	1	2	3
5	4	2	3	4	5
1	2		4	2	0

LETTERBLOCKS

Move the letterblocks around so that words are formed on top and below that you can associate with Elton John. In one block, the letter from the top row has been switched with the letter from the bottom row.

★★ Sudoku X

Fill in the grid so that each row, each column and each 3 x 3 frame contains every number from 1 to 9. The two main diagonals of the grid also contain every number from 1 to 9.

9	5	7	4	6			3	8	
			5	1				2	
						7			
	6	3				5			
	4		1	3		8			
		8	9						
	3	6							
7		1		4					
		3							

CONNECT TWO

An oxymoron is a combination of seemingly contradictory or incongruous words, such as "science fiction"(science means "knowledge or study dealing with facts or truth" while fiction means "an imagined or invented creation"). Connect the words with meanings that oppose each other and make oxymorons.

BAGGY	FRESH
CANNED	RESULTS
INITIAL	UGLY
PRETTY	TIGHTS

★★★ Presidential Losers by Don Law

ACROSS

1 Marjoram, e.g.
5 It may need dusting
9 Men of wisdom
14 Director/producer Kazan
15 Arrowrock Dam's river
16 Rhone tributary
17 1936 loser to Roosevelt
19 Narrow groove
20 Sunburn aftermath
21 Take away from
23 Willow tree
25 Collation
26 Persuade
29 1957 Buddy Holly hit
33 Matchless
34 Secret observers
35 Swing to and ___
36 Kickoff shouts
37 One going downhill fast
38 Marinate
39 K-O connection
40 Rotates
41 Maestro Koussevitzky
42 One of these days
44 Comic Howie
45 The McCoys, for one
46 "Light My Fire" group
48 Spotted
51 Alberta expanse
55 Beyond angry
56 1800 loser to Jefferson
58 *The Tempest* sprite
59 Some are bagged
60 Encumbrance
61 Barry Manilow hit
62 Dull pain
63 Mana of tennis

DOWN

1 Trouble quantity?
2 Covergirl Macpherson
3 In widespread use
4 Swells up
5 Journalist Chung
6 Blue ___ Mountains
7 Spanish bear
8 Remain unresolved
9 *Hannah and Her ___* (1986)
10 Off the path
11 1976 loser to Carter
12 "Layla" singer Clapton
13 Rush-hour subway rarity
18 Supermarket section
22 Kuwaiti royal
24 Kvetched
26 Sagan and Sandburg
27 Southwest poplar
28 2008 loser to Obama
30 Struggles
31 ___ *in Harlem* (1991)
32 Hayseed
34 No-fat milk
37 Lackey's lack
38 Well-thought-out
40 Majestic
41 Plastic wrap
43 Gleeful
44 Filled with gloom
47 Dr. Phil's mentor
48 Neeson in *Rob Roy*
49 Odd, in Dundee
50 Lab findings
52 Wrack's partner
53 All het up
54 Composer Dohnányi
57 DOE predecessor: Abbr.

★ BrainSnack®—Chime the Bells

Which bell makes a sound that differs from the other sounds?

LETTER LINE

Put a letter in each of the squares below to make a word which means "AN AUTHORITY." The number clues refer to other words which can be made from the whole.

2 1 5 9 10 3 CHANGES; 7 2 10 7 5 9 CRAZY PEOPLE;
3 4 2 1 1 5 6 STUTTER; 3 4 6 2 9 10 THREAD;
3 1 2 6 4 5 9 SPRUCE UP

1	2	3	4	5	6	7	8	9	10

★ Word Pyramid

Each word in the pyramid has the letters of the word above it, plus a new letter.

D
(1) one tenth of a meter
(2) dense
(3) female domestic
(4) tools used to store and deliver information
(5) crown
(6) looked up to
(7) ended threat

WORD SHRINKS

Make each word shorter by taking away one letter at a time but keeping the remaining letters in their original order and form a new word. Do this as many times as possible, forming a new word as each letter is deleted. Example : PLATE ➡ LATE ➡ ATE ➡ AT

WAIST

★★ Sunny Weather

Where will the sun shine? With the knowledge that each arrow points to a place where a symbol should be, can you locate the sunny spots? The symbols cannot be next to each other vertically, horizontally or diagonally. A symbol cannot be placed on top of an arrow. We show one symbol.

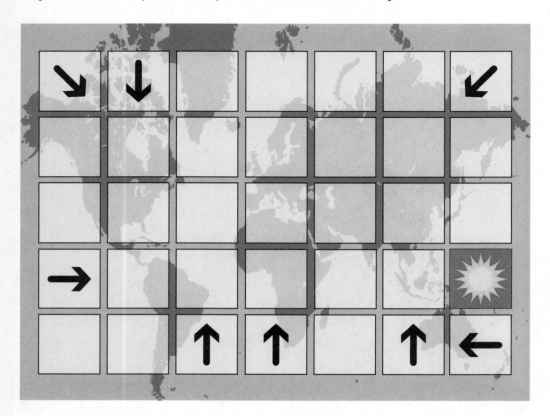

DOUBLETALK

Homophones are words that share the same pronunciation, no matter how they are spelled. If they are spelled differently then they are called heterographs. Find heterographs meaning:

PART OF A CONTRACT and ANIMAL FINGERS

★★★★ Themeless by Karen Peterson

ACROSS

1 *The Sound of Music* baroness
5 Lugged around
10 Divests
14 Friend of Androcles
15 Russian skier Smetanina
16 "___ penny ... hot cross buns"
17 Pixar parent
19 Ring up
20 Whole
21 *Quantum Leap* star Scott
23 Bluejackets
24 Bearing weapons
25 *Help!* and *Revolver*
26 Glade
29 Saves for later viewing
32 Ballpark instrument
33 Maker of tiny combs
34 "How sad!"
35 Fishing spot
36 Reunion group
37 Male Gypsy
38 Not loaded
39 Quarterback Favre
40 Run circles around
42 West in *Myra Breckinridge*
43 Like dead weight
44 Huaraches
48 Antipasto meat
50 Watchtower guard
51 Confess
52 Small
54 Indy driver Luyendyk
55 Two-___(hockey advantage)
56 Oklahoma tribe
57 She was wild about Harry
58 Pianist Williams
59 Position

DOWN

1 Cary in *The Princess Bride*
2 Climbing vine
3 Conductor Georg (1912–97)
4 Caribbean islands
5 Prosecutors
6 Malt kilns
7 Bitty
8 Suffix for Peking
9 Sunup
10 Boston chair
11 Like silent alarms
12 Wooded valley
13 Room in *la casa*
18 Doesn't keep from slipping
22 "Measure of ___": Clay Aiken
24 *Luck and Pluck* author
26 Stalker, e.g.
27 Well-groomed
28 Fella
29 Source of poi
30 Ballplayer Moises
31 "Sweethearts Dance" singer
32 Satellite's path
35 Restricted air lane
36 IOU holder
38 Part of a poppy
39 African language family
41 Reptiles not found in New Zealand
42 Behavior
44 Rive Gauche sight
45 Ekberg in *4 for Texas*
46 1971 Elton John hit
47 Shiny and smooth
48 Wild guess
49 Lake Thun's river
50 Sky blight
53 Rescuer of Odysseus

★★ Sudoku Twin

Fill in the grid so that each row, each column and each 3 x 3 frame contains every number from 1 to 9. A sudoku twin is two connected 9 x 9 sudokus.

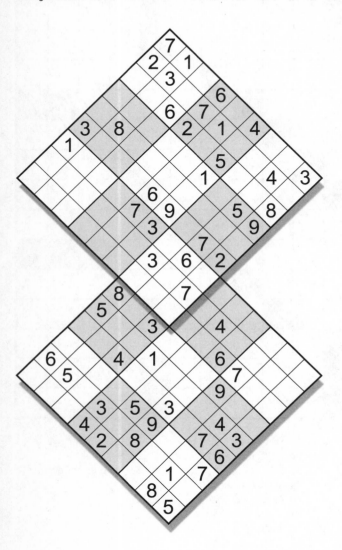

LETTERBLOCKS

Move the letterblocks around so that words are formed on top and below that you can associate with energy.

★★★ **Futoshiki**

Fill in the 5 x 5 grid with the numbers from 1 to 5 once per row and column, while following the greater than/lesser than symbols shown. There is only one valid solution that can be reached through logic and clear thinking alone!

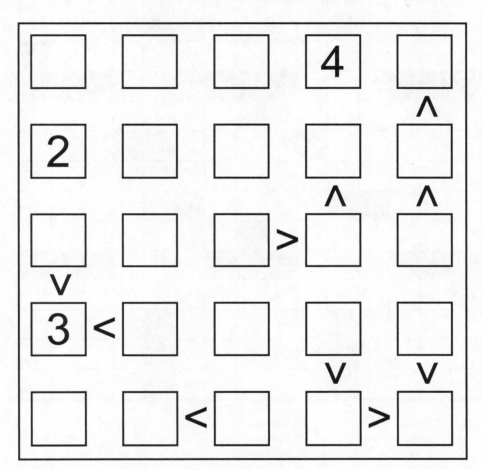

ONE LETTER LESS OR MORE

The word on the right side contains the letters of the word on the left side plus or minus the letter in the middle. One letter is already in the right place.

D E C E A S E D -E ☐ ☐ ☐ A ☐ ☐ ☐

★★★★ Born on Christmas Day by John M. Samson

ACROSS

1 Paul Bunyan's ox
5 Not stay cool
10 Pianist Gilels
14 Jones of talk radio
15 Sacred Hindu text
16 Senior lobby
17 Totally unexciting
18 Festival in Adar
19 Gosling in *The Ides of March*
20 Scientist born on Christmas Day
23 "Boogie Woogie Bugle ___"
24 "Go team!"
25 Highest naval rank
29 Vending machine drink
33 "T-R-O-U-B-L-E" singer Travis
34 *Fiesque* composer
36 River inlet
37 Singer born on Christmas Day
41 Back in time
42 Sunday assent
43 Nerve networks
44 Firenze locale
47 Silo
49 Apparent path of the sun
50 Rocks in the drink
51 Actor born on Christmas Day
59 Waterproof cover
60 "___ Meenie": Kingston and Bieber
61 Without ___ (broke)
62 Temper tantrum
63 *Die Hard 2* director Harlin
64 Honeybunch
65 Flanders river
66 Mead's *Coming ___ in Samoa*
67 Become worthy of

DOWN

1 Streisand's nickname
2 "___ Wanna Do": Sheryl Crow
3 Financial pessimist
4 Further evidence
5 Melonlike tropical fruit
6 Madrid water
7 Figure in a bust
8 "Sounds good to me!"
9 Nigeria neighbor
10 Kitt who was Catwoman
11 BLT option
12 Locale of Tabriz
13 TLC giver
21 Kinda
22 Gum glob
25 Looking for a hit
26 *Rocky IV* boxer
27 Some MoMA holdings
28 Spitting animal
29 Street talk
30 ___-porter (ready-to-wear)
31 Carrier of crude
32 ___-walsy
35 "Botch-___" (1952 hit)
38 Córdoba cattleman
39 Sky dragon
40 Rebel
45 Slide-on RV
46 A Dada founder
48 Steakhouse order
51 2011 FedEx Cup winner
52 Recommend earnestly
53 Boating hazard
54 Sicilian resort
55 Opera soprano Huang
56 Out of port
57 *The Lion King* sound
58 Swivel
59 Go for it

★★★ BrainSnack®—Ghost Invader

Which ghost (1–7) doesn't belong in this cemetery?

BLOCK ANAGRAM

Form the word that is described in the brackets with the letters above the grid. An extra letter is already in the right place.

WEST GIRL (hand-to-hand combat)

							N	

★★★ Concentration—Translation

Can you solve the calculation below without writing anything down?

How much is 1/4 of 1/2 of 2^3 divided by 1/2 of the result?

CHANGELINGS

Each of the three lines of letters below spell a word that has a medical connection, but the letters have been mixed up. Four letters from the first word are now in the third line, four letters from the third word are in the second line and four letters from the second word are in the first line. The remaining letters are in their original places. What are the words?

```
A Q R I A I O T I E
D U A P S N T I N O
N E T R E B S I C N
```

★★★★ Sue Grafton's Alphabet I by John McCarthy

ACROSS

1 Trimming target
5 Summoned to the lobby
10 Attend Andover
14 Singer who's an actress
15 Stag, at a party
16 Bring on board
17 For ___ and a day
18 Hook
19 Thompson of *Wit*
20 Sue Grafton's "D"
22 No picnic
24 Audrey's *Charade* costar
25 Type of ID
26 They're great conductors
29 Sue Grafton's "E"
33 O'Hara's ___ *to Live*
34 Charon's dwarf planet
35 Bedbound
36 Tag with a "PG-13"
37 Soccer highlights
38 Rural delivery?
39 *Rugrats* dad
40 "___ Baby": Eartha Kitt
41 Aida's native land
42 Sue Grafton's "H"
44 "Lucille" singer Kenny
45 Pen men
46 Garr with a *Tootsie* role
47 Prison guards, slangily
50 Marinara ingredients
54 Captain of fiction
55 Banded mineral
57 Mosque prayer leader
58 Shell food?
59 Trojan War account
60 Ming artifact
61 Cameo stone
62 Hand cart
63 Big name in Art Deco

DOWN

1 Took to one's heels
2 Diana Krall album ___ *Scenes*
3 Vicinity
4 Tweety's home
5 Indiana NBA team
6 Set at ease
7 Fall guy
8 Printing measures
9 S&L transactions
10 Racine tragedy
11 Hoarfrost
12 Humorist Bombeck
13 Tintinnabulate
21 Cotton bundle
23 Start over from scratch
25 Tonsil neighbor
26 Waterlogged ground

27 Muse of erotic poetry
28 Ryan's daughter
29 Gladden greatly
30 Mythical weeper
31 "___ de Lune": Debussy
32 Fitzgerald and Raines
34 Fishing holes
37 Denied
38 Sue Grafton's "F"
40 Refuse transporter
41 *The Thin Man* wife
43 Cooling chest
44 Cure
46 Kind of recall
47 1974 Peace Prize winner
48 *The Medallion* star Jackie
49 Off-color

50 Bovine flyswatter
51 Sharif in *The Last Templar*
52 Dawn's direction
53 *Peter Pan* pirate
56 Day-___ paint

★★ Keep Going

Start on a blank square of your choice and connect as many blank squares as possible with one single continuous line. You can only connect squares along vertical and horizontal lines, not along diagonal lines. You must continue the connecting line up until the next obstacle, i.e., the rim of the box, a black square or a square that has already been used. You can change direction at any obstacle you meet. Each square can be used only once. The number of blank squares that will be left unused is marked in the upper square. There is more than one solution. We show only one solution.

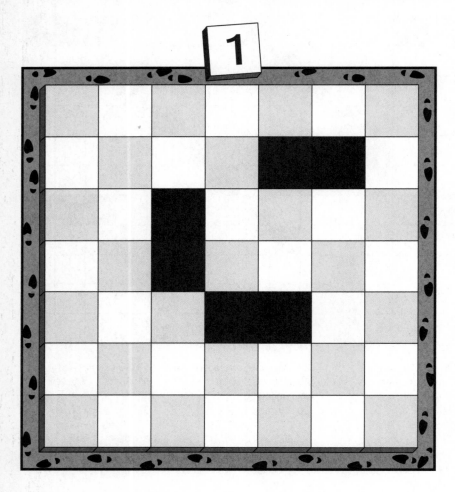

UNCANNY TURN

Rearrange the letters of the phrase below to form a cognate anagram, one which is related or connected in meaning to the original phrase. The answer can be one or more words.

ONCE FRUIT

★ Fire Department

All the words are hidden vertically, horizontally or diagonally—in both directions. The letters that remain unused form a sentence from left to right.

```
T H E W A T E R C A N N O N F
I R E D T E P A E L Y R T M E
T A E S H R N T L D L H A S A
H T I E G E R A U P D I A R E
H O R N I S C T U O R A R C U
H O I C L C S M S W E T L D G
R L U C G U P M T D E T Y N A
U S R E N E T E C E T G T E L
H E R O I S M D E R N O E M P
S E M N H S U I F I U F F O C
R R R E S S M C N D L L A W O
E M O O A O R I I O O O S T N
V H F H L C A N S W V O O O T
I P I E F R L E I N E D R A A
D T N L T I A R D T O I N W I
I T U M H A M I O I N N G S N
C O D E R E D S T M O G T H E
E R S T T H E P O E L I C E R
```

DOWNTIME
DRILL
FLASHING LIGHT
FLOODING
HELMET
HEROISM
HORN
LADDER
MEDICINE
PLAGUE
POWDER
PUMP
RESCUE
SAFETY
SEAT
SIREN
STUDY
TOOLS
TRAINING
UNIFORM
VOLUNTEER
WATER CANNON
WOMEN

ALARM
CALL

CODE RED
CONTAINER

DISINFECT
DIVERS

SANDWICH

What five-letter word belongs between the word on the left and the word on the right, so that the first and second word, and the second and third word, each form a common compound word or phrase?

SCORE _ _ _ _ _ WALK

★★★★ Sue Grafton's Alphabet II by John McCarthy

ACROSS

1 Summer place
5 Onward
10 Unparalleled
14 Locality
15 Go edgewise
16 McBeal or Sheedy
17 Tenterhook
18 Get a whiff of
19 Give it up
20 Sue Grafton's "I"
22 Native Alaskan
24 Too-too
25 Snicker-___ (old knife)
26 Libra
29 Sue Grafton's "U"
33 Dull finish
34 Get gussied up
35 Spanish pronoun
36 Moneychanger's fee
37 Pumped up
38 Whiskered barker
39 "Shiny Happy People" band
40 1994 Indy 500 winner
41 Fencing thrust
42 Sue Grafton's "T"
44 Lifts
45 Cuba Libre wedge
46 Vibraphonist Jackson
47 Carla in Spy Kids
50 Sue Grafton's "R"
54 Writer Bagnold
55 Urban insect
57 "Another Pyramid" musical
58 Primrose path
59 Accustom
60 Kane's Rosebud
61 Boris Godunov, e.g.
62 One of the Cyclades
63 Volcano in Sicily

DOWN

1 "What ___ say?"
2 Donegal island
3 Chicken chow ___
4 Home of Stanford University
5 Useful qualities
6 Equine hybrid
7 Cut and splice
8 1980s sitcom alien
9 Lawyer in court, often
10 Sponsor
11 Giantess who wrestled Thor
12 Close angrily
13 Keyboard goof
21 Saskatchewan native
23 Watched
25 Sinister smile
26 Brainy
27 One on the rebound?
28 Grisham's ___ to Kill
29 Drives
30 Taylor Swift fans
31 Ornamental orange
32 Cardiff locale
34 Rarely used anymore
37 Taken with
38 It might be X-rayed
40 ___ arms (agitated)
41 Fiesque composer
43 Breaking ball
44 Fortune
46 Prefix for manage
47 Cabbage
48 Some, in Spain
49 Gershon in Showgirls
50 Fidel Castro's brother
51 Sword handle
52 Bob Dylan's "Gates of ___"
53 "I did it!"
56 Pepsi diet drink

★★★ Sport Maze

Draw the shortest way from the ball to the goal. You can only move along vertical and horizontal lines, not along diagonal lines. The figure on each square indicates the number of squares the ball must be moved in the same direction. You can change direction at each stop.

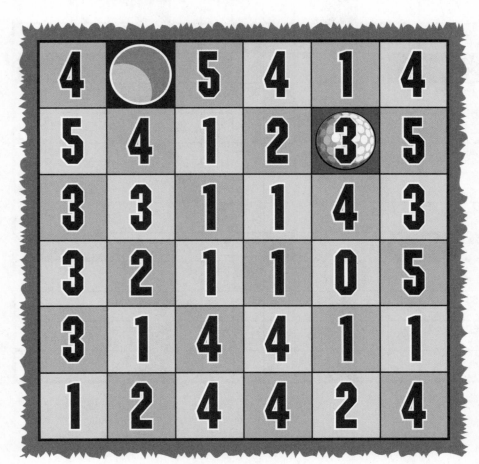

DOODLE PUZZLE

A doodle puzzle is a combination of images, letters and/or numbers that represent a word or a concept. If you cannot solve a doodle puzzle, do not look at the answer right away. Think hard—and outside the box.

★★★★ Sue Grafton's Alphabet III by John McCarthy

ACROSS

1 Henrique of hockey
5 ___ and bounds
10 Japanese beef
14 *A Raisin in the Sun* heroine
15 Martini drop-in
16 Tennis player Andreev
17 "You're making ___ mistake!"
18 Insomniac's need
19 Shakespearean king
20 Sue Grafton's "S"
22 Sue Grafton's "L"
24 "Bleeding Love" singer Lewis
26 Dawn Chong in *The Alibi*
27 Sue Grafton's "O"
30 Boardroom VIP
35 Sweet ___ College
36 "T-R-O-U-B-L-E" singer Travis
37 Yoko in *Let It Be*
38 First Alaska governor
39 Julianne in *Freedomland*
40 *Ice Age* sabertooth
41 Celtic sea god
42 Weeper of myth
43 Swansea locale
44 Columbus sponsor
46 Saying
47 Pal of Pooh and Piglet
48 Shire in *Windows*
50 Get some air
54 Sue Grafton's "G"
58 Storm systems
59 Edward James in *Blade Runner*
61 Greek goddess of wine
62 Act as accomplice
63 Oyster shell lining
64 Quilt size
65 Not his
66 Nobelist writer Canetti
67 Aardvark's dinner

DOWN

1 "How sad!"
2 Mazar in *Batman Forever*
3 Indigo plant
4 Portuguese explorer
5 Gorky Park locale
6 Pompeo of *Grey's Anatomy*
7 Neckwear
8 Daredevil Knievel
9 Split
10 Sue Grafton's "K"
11 Eastern arch
12 Fluffy wraps
13 Boots a ground ball
21 Within earshot
23 Be on standby
25 Cirque du Soleil performer
27 Reference marks
28 Some are irresistible
29 Jeweled crown
31 Enlarge the staff
32 Do-re-mi
33 Texas Hold'em stakes
34 Sue Grafton's "N"
36 Cat's-paw
39 Sue Grafton detective
40 Gulf of Mexico city
42 Eye source in *Macbeth*
43 Fanciful desire
45 Acts the blowhard
46 Positive aspects
49 Where Socrates shopped
50 Rainy day feeling
51 Housecoat
52 Fancy pitcher
53 Mideast airline
55 Shaped with an ax
56 "I'll get right ___"
57 Eternities
60 DL + DLI

★ Spot the Differences

Find the nine differences in the image on the right.

DOUBLETALK

Homophones are words that share the same pronunciation, no matter how they are spelled. If they are spelled differently then they are called heterographs. Find heterographs meaning:

APTITUDE and A RESCUE ROCKET

★★★ Sudoku

Fill in the grid so that each row, each column and each 3 x 3 frame contains every number from 1 to 9.

					3			
	8		9		2			
1		4						
		5	4					3
9			3			7		
	3							6
		3	1			4		
	9			2	8		3	
	5						6	8

LETTERBLOCKS

Move the letterblocks around so that words are formed on top and below that you can associate with kitchenware. In some blocks, the letter from the top row has been switched with the letter from the bottom row.

I M S P E R M
A T S K L A U

★★ Word Sudoku

Complete the grid so that each row, each column and each 3 x 3 frame contains the nine letters from the black box below. The hidden nine-letter word is in the diagonal from top left to bottom right.

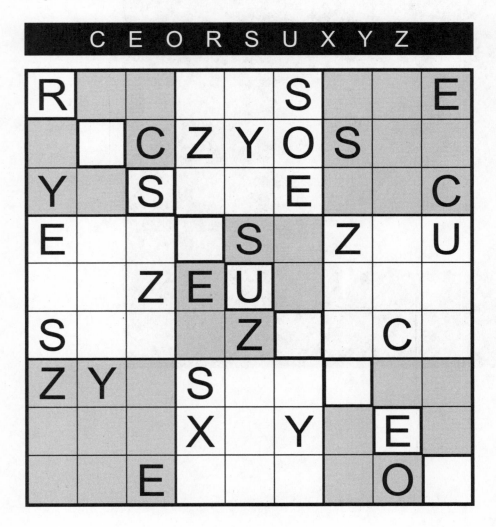

C E O R S U X Y Z

FRIENDS?

What do the following words have in common?

BE HARD SOFT KITCHEN SILVER TABLE

★★ BrainSnack®—Masquerade

Which color (1–10) should replace the question mark?

CONNECT TWO

An oxymoron is a combination of seemingly contradictory or incongruous words, such as "science fiction"(science means "knowledge or study dealing with facts or truth" while fiction means "an imagined or invented creation"). Connect the words with meanings that oppose each other and make oxymorons.

CALCULATED   SOUND
COUNTLESS   BABY
MUTE   RISK
BIG   NUMBERS

★★★★ Pretty Fishy by Tim Wagner

ACROSS

1 Arctic reindeer herder
5 Barber's accessory
10 Unwanted e-mail
14 Noodle concoction?
15 *The Devil Wears ___* (2006)
16 General's staffer
17 One trying to land a game fish?
19 Stats for Rocky
20 Feats of conceit
21 Mother from Albania
23 Skin wounds
24 Star sopranos
25 Wife of Amen-Ra
26 Gave a postgame report
29 Went parabolically
32 Prevents publication of
33 Inventor Whitney
34 Locale of Luang Prabang
35 "Easy Street" musical
36 "Royal" nuisance
37 E. Holder et al.
38 Major European lake
39 Rock rabbits
40 L and M, at times
42 Barbie's guy
43 ___ *Right, Jack* (1959)
44 Something to eat with a cocktail?
48 "___ done!" ("Good job!")
50 Head scarf
51 Fish story
52 Clairvoyant fish?
54 "Gracious me!"
55 Prefix with mural or party
56 Father of Cordelia
57 Santa's workshop products
58 Judicial suspensions
59 Whirling current

DOWN

1 Tabloid lawyer's worry
2 Aphorism
3 Change at Chihuahua
4 Diversions
5 Wood strip
6 Stings, essentially
7 Liotta and Walston
8 Poetic tribute
9 Proton or electron
10 Petty tyrant
11 Height of walleye season?
12 Stirs
13 Arizona city
18 Standing tall
22 Perón and Gabor
24 Nora Ephron's sister
26 Saturn features
27 "Ellistoniana" essayist
28 Big rackets
29 Moonwalker Shepard
30 Brand of spaghetti sauce
31 Enormous devilfish?
32 Mournful sound
35 Psychotherapy
36 Highest point
38 Vocal
39 Concealed
41 Corrects copy
42 Dorothy's home
44 Comedian Shandling
45 Readied the presses
46 "Slammin' Sammy" of golf
47 Wizard pal of Hermione
48 Duma vote
49 Shakespearean villain
50 Alpha follower
53 Treebeard in *LOTR*

★ Hourglass

Starting in the middle, each word in the top half has the letters of the word below it, plus a new letter, and each word in the bottom half has the letters of the word above it, plus a new letter.

(1) bays
(2) songs
(3) rapid discharge of firearms
(4) egg-shaped
(5) have a great affection for
(6) important food and source of oil
(7) purple
(8) fierce

SANDWICH

What three-letter word belongs between the word on the left and the word on the right, so that the first and second word, and the second and third word, each form a common compound word or phrase?

SOME _ _ _ TIME

★★ Horoscope

Fill in the grid so that every row, every column and every frame of six boxes contains six different symbols: health, work, money, happiness, family and love. Look at the row or column that corresponds with your sign of the zodiac and find out which of the six symbols are important for you today. The symbols appear in increasing order of importance (1–6). It's up to you to translate the meaning of each symbol to your specific situation.

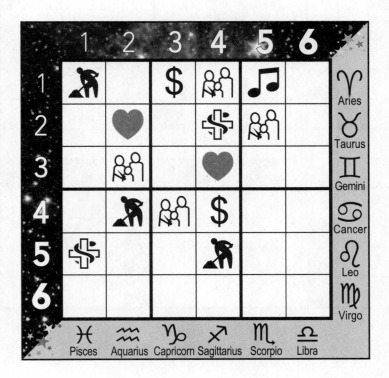

UNCANNY TURN

Rearrange the letters of the phrase below to form a cognate anagram, one which is related or connected in meaning to the original phrase. The answer can be one or more words.

SLID THERE

★★★★ Themeless by Karen Peterson

ACROSS

1 "Jabberwocky" is one
5 "To err is ___ ..."
10 Put one's foot down?
14 *Born Free* lioness
15 Japanese port
16 Heraldic wreath
17 Like excellent corned beef
18 Irish-born poet Tate
19 "The Last ___ of Summer"
20 Ill-bred
22 Buttinski
24 Jacuzzi sigh
25 Track part
26 Breastbone
30 African Peace Nobelist
33 *No Country for Old Men* setting
34 "Chasing Pavements" singer
36 Hankering
37 Take note of
38 Loses enthusiasm
39 They outrank specialists: Abbr.
40 Rarebit ingredient
41 Pass up
42 Lane in *Untraceable*
43 Drink with an olive
45 Noncombatant
47 "___ on the roof ..." ("Your Song" lyric)
48 French sea
49 Swiftest cat
52 Grant pardon for
56 Peewee
57 *Monte* ___ (2011)
59 Urge
60 C shapes
61 Grove members
62 Ex of Tiger Woods
63 Musical club
64 Boxcars
65 Governess

DOWN

1 ___-mell
2 It might be in a tub
3 Abraham's grandson
4 Devilfish
5 Japan's largest island
6 "Industry" state
7 ___-jongg
8 Calla lily, for one
9 Numbers
10 Morally degraded
11 Vienna rail vehicle
12 "You're something ___!"
13 Equal
21 Woosnam and Fleming
23 Jutland citizen
26 Power source
27 Motors of Palo Alto
28 "The best teacher"
29 New Zealand aborigine
30 Crenshaw or casaba
31 "I Will Be" singer Lewis
32 Sierra Club patron Adams
35 Dandie Dinmont, e.g.
38 Alternatives to glasses
39 80% of the atmosphere
41 Italian car
42 Member's payment
44 Tropical fly
46 Decorate fancily
49 Cliff rock
50 Pitch
51 Mata of espionage
52 Aweather antonym
53 *Damn Yankees* temptress
54 Futile
55 Pulitzer winner Ferber
58 *Toy Story* dino

★ Opera

All the words are hidden vertically, horizontally or diagonally—in both directions. The letters that remain unused form a sentence from left to right.

```
T J A N A C E K A T R O T O W
A E E M E H T C K E O P R R A
M R N B E R L I O Z E R A A G
O B I O A U L I K I C E Z T N
N R T A R O G M M B Y O O O E
T I B M Y T H O L O G Y M R R
E T Y T N H O L L E H T O I E
V T H C E R B W H A P O I O C
E E S I M A E M U S I L I C R
R N A N R O S S I N I D A L I
D P R I A O D A O C U C T Y G
I I O C C N W I L P I T H R O
G L U C K M H O C E M G K M L
N U S U I C E A I N U O A T E
O O H P E F O L N R A Z C R T
S D R A M A M T O D N A R U T
O R A M E A U F I D E A N A O
O P E B A L L A D E Y L R A Z
```

BRITTEN
CARMEN
COMIC
COMPOSER
DIALOGUE
DRAMA
GLUCK
HANDEL
JANACEK
MELODY
MONTEVERDI
MOZART
MYTHOLOGY
NORMA
ORATORIO
OTHELLO
PLAY
PUCCINI
RAMEAU
RIGOLETTO
ROSSINI
SONG
TENOR
THEME
TRAGIC
TURANDOT
WAGNER
ZARZUELA

AIDA
ARIA
BALLADE
BERLIOZ
BIZET
BRECHT

REPOSITION PREPOSITION

Unscramble OFF OR DRAW and find a two-word preposition.

★★★ Binairo

Complete the grid with zeros and ones until there are 5 zeros and 6 ones in every row and every column. No more than two of the same number can be next to or under each other. Rows or columns with exactly the same content are not allowed. There is only one valid solution.

		1			▼					
							1			
1			1	1			1		0	
	1									
					1				1	
▶		1		1	1				1	◀
			1		1		1			
		0				0		1		
				0						
				0		0	0		0	
	0	0			▲				0	

ONE LETTER LESS OR MORE

The word on the right side contains the letters of the word on the left side plus or minus the letter in the middle. One letter is already in the right place.

K I N G F I S H -K ☐ ☐ S ☐ ☐ ☐ ☐

★★★★ Punny Business by John McCarthy

ACROSS

1 Take it easy
5 Steel girder
9 Tremulous tree
14 *Sesame Street* Muppet
15 Pack animal
16 French textiles city
17 Matty of baseball
18 Stuffy
19 Stonewall
20 So-so food?
22 *The ___ Network* (2010)
23 Snack in a shell
24 Ohio metropolis
25 Stand up for (oneself)
28 Slapstick prop
31 More recent
32 Sophia in *Arabesque*
33 Leary's drug
34 ___ Shan mountains
35 Wine grape
36 Low-lying area
37 *Charlotte's Web* horse
38 Muscle power
39 Napery
40 Vacation rentals
42 Sacred choral works
43 Mahler's ___ *of a Wayfarer*
44 Max Ernst's movement
45 Substantially made
47 Female mob inductee?
51 River of Tours
52 Lexicon entry
53 "Tell ___ the judge!"
54 The slim picture
55 Healthy
56 Oak abode
57 Take a shot
58 "___ unrelated note ..."
59 The Red and the Dead

DOWN

1 Canadian emblem
2 Jalisco water jar
3 Mine, to Mimi
4 Bob Cousy's retired number
5 Effect
6 Pack animal
7 "That's ___!" ("Not so!")
8 "Radio Song" group
9 Derby laggard
10 Funny TV series
11 No-frills jet?
12 Scat queen Fitzgerald
13 *The Haunting* heroine
21 Jamie of *M*A*S*H*
22 Sport using a clay disk
24 One-way sign
25 Prank
26 Japanese watch
27 Lovely honeymoon lodging?
28 Roadwork markers
29 Key
30 Gardens of delight
32 Actors may be fed them
35 "Little" digit
36 A and B, e.g.
38 Chicken colonel?
39 Vein glory
41 Bon Jovi drummer
42 Incense
44 *Our Gang* girl
45 Remains at a steel mill
46 Popular vegan food
47 Complainer's sound
48 Suited to ___
49 "___ Most Unusual Day"
50 Pixels
52 *Horton Hears a ___!* (2008)

★★★ Sport Maze

Draw the shortest way from the ball to the goal. You can only move along vertical and horizontal lines, not along diagonal lines. The figure on each square indicates the number of squares the ball must be moved in the same direction. You can change direction at each stop.

1	4	5	1	4	4
5	4	1	3	4	3
3	2	3	3	4	2
1	3	1	●	3	5
2	2	1	4	0	2
3	1	4	3	1	2

BLOCK ANAGRAM

Form the words that are described in the brackets with the letters above the grid. Extra letters are already in the right place.

NYC GLACIER (engaging in contests on two wheels)

B				C						I		

★★ Kakuro

Each number in a black area is the sum of the numbers that you have to enter in the next empty boxes beside or below. The empty boxes that make up the sum are called a run. The sum of the across run is written above the diagonal in the black area and the sum of the down run is written below the diagonal. Runs can only contain the numbers 1 through 9 and each number in a run can only be used once. The gray boxes contain only odd numbers and the white only even numbers.

DOODLE PUZZLE

A doodle puzzle is a combination of images, letters and/or numbers that represent a word or a concept. If you cannot solve a doodle puzzle, do not look at the answer right away. Think hard—and outside the box.

★★★★ Themeless by Karen Peterson

ACROSS
1 Jersey baby
5 Globe representation
10 Noodlehead
14 Shape runners are attracted to
15 Rutger of *Blade Runner*
16 Reveler's cry, in ancient Rome
17 McEntire of country
18 River from the Savoy Alps
19 Bop on the head
20 Kicked upstairs
22 Causes consternation
24 Major steps
25 *Clash by Night* playwright
26 Bread in an Indian restaurant
27 *It's A Gift* star
30 Like Heidi Klum
33 Fruit of forgetfulness
34 Broad foot size
35 Suffix for buck
36 In a wild state
37 Dido's "Life for ___"
38 Zip, in soccer
39 Judge played by Stallone
40 3-D feature
41 Mechanical men
43 Stylish dresser
44 Subsides
45 Marvel
49 Happy hunting grounds
51 Guy Fawkes Night sights
52 Objecting to
53 Parasitic loafer
55 Multiple curls, e.g.
56 Egyptian sun god
57 Catalogs
58 Electric sword
59 Saharan
60 America's Cup racer
61 Laura in *Rambling Rose*

DOWN
1 Part of USMC
2 Steer away from
3 Car repair cost
4 Pink bird
5 Bleach can do it
6 Gardens amidst the sands
7 Wept over
8 Irish sea god
9 Appalling
10 Oral contest
11 Catch too many Zs
12 Desirable soil
13 Perfect gymnastic scores
21 Jazz vocalist Anita
23 Aloha Day neckwear
25 Heptad plus one
27 Lexicon listings

28 Jalopy ding
29 Adam and Eve's youngest
30 "Sweater Girl" Turner
31 Emerald Isle
32 1964 loser to Johnson
33 British textile center
36 Welcoming
37 Good as new
39 Through
40 Tim Conway character
42 Steep-sided valley
43 Surpassing in quality
45 One is named after Mars
46 Parisian pancake
47 Social outcast
48 German steel city
49 2011 FedEx Cup winner

50 Düsseldorf duck
51 Long-neck pear
54 Fjord's kin

★★★ BrainSnack®—Target Practice

Which target (1–6) differs from all the rest?

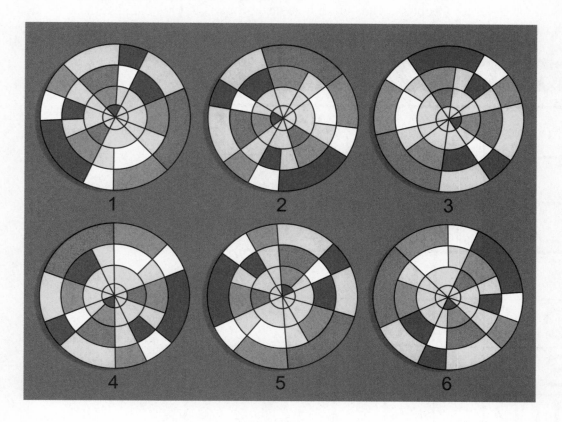

1

2

3

4

5

6

DOUBLETALK

Homophones are words that share the same pronunciation, no matter how they are spelled. If they are spelled differently then they are called heterographs. Find heterographs meaning:

SEVEN IN A ROW and LACKING STRENGTH

★ Word Sudoku

Complete the grid so that each row, each column and each 3 x 3 frame contains the nine letters from the black box below. The hidden nine-letter word is in the diagonal from top left to bottom right.

D	E	I	L	P	R	S	U	Y
S			L			Y		E
								P
	L	R	I					U
E				L				Y
	D	I		R				
L	S					U		
	I	P						
			D			R		
			Y					

ONE LETTER LESS OR MORE

The word on the right side contains the letters of the word on the left side plus or minus the letter in the middle. One letter is already in the right place.

| D | E | C | I | M | A | L | S | +P | | I | | | | | | |

★★★ BrainSnack®—Windy Hill

On which hill (A–E) is the windmill in the wrong place?

UNCANNY TURN

Rearrange the letters of the phrase below to form a cognate anagram, one which is related or connected in meaning to the original phrase. The answer can be one or more words.

SEEN AS MIST

★★★★ Themeless by Karen Peterson

ACROSS

1 Venus de Milo's lack
5 Perfectly vertical
10 Cut class
14 Ill-gotten gains
15 Hawaiian porch
16 Wash up
17 Highly spiced stew
18 Provide income for
19 Jones in *American Virgin*
20 Andalusian dance
22 Norton in *The Illusionist*
24 Cellulose eater
25 Kingdom
26 Suffix for green
27 Japanese hot-pot dish
30 "___ the Champions": Queen
33 Plays bonspiel
34 British omega
35 Horned goddess
36 Incursion
37 Inflamed
38 *Car Talk* network
39 Melody enhancement
40 Uranus has 15
41 Dvorak's *New World*
43 London's Old ___
44 Alda and Bates
45 Makes bubbly
49 Far East
51 Cruz in *Nine*
52 Kunis in *Black Swan*
53 Like neon or argon
55 Virna in *The Heist*
56 The Red Baron et al.
57 Like a poltergeist
58 Wellington's alma mater
59 Network terminal
60 Given an "NC-17"
61 Unit of force

DOWN

1 In the sky
2 Esther of *Good Times*
3 Back tooth
4 Stutters
5 Superabundance
6 Jousting spear
7 Invalidate
8 Long March leader
9 Every 14 days
10 Inchmeal
11 Michigan city
12 "Match King" Kreuger
13 Remain unsettled
21 Tipperary locale
23 Podium
25 Bucolic
27 Irascible
28 *Show Boat* composer
29 Caesar's fateful time
30 Advances to the finals
31 Catch a look at
32 Went *par avion*
33 Mint products
36 Undeveloped area
37 Self-styled
39 Comparer's word
40 Slush
42 Gratify
43 Blew off steam
45 Lofty home
46 Hoity-___
47 Big name in printers
48 Le Pont-Neuf spans it
49 Arabian sultanate
50 *Hannah Montana* character
51 Cute and sassy
54 Instructive org.

★★★ Sudoku X

Fill in the grid so that each row, each column and each 3 x 3 frame contains every number from 1 to 9. The two main diagonals of the grid also contain every number from 1 to 9.

								2
			1		9	4		
	4				3			
				3				9
	3	4				5	6	
6	1						4	8
				8			5	
		6	9		7			
4		7					2	3

SANDWICH

What four-letter word belongs between the word on the left and the word on the right, so that the first and second word, and the second and third word, each form a common compound word or phrase?

SAND _ _ _ _ ROLL

★ Safe Code

To open the safe you have to replace the question mark with the correct figure. You can find this figure by determining the logical methods behind the numbers shown. These methods can include calculation, inversion, repetition, chronological succession, forming ascending and descending series.

SAFE A08

CHANGE ONE, CHANGE ANOTHER

Change one letter in the first word to create a second word, then change one letter in the second word to create a third word which will become the final word by changing one letter. There may be more than one possible answer.

FORK ➡ _ _ _ _ ➡ _ _ _ _ ➡ FINE

★★★★★ Big Words I by John M. Samson

ACROSS

1 Homes to squirrels
5 Passover feast
10 Click-on image
14 Football foul
15 Make amends
16 Spanish cat
17 Pitchfork prong
18 "Is ___ dagger which I see ...": Shak.
19 Noncoms
20 Foolish
22 Very particular
24 Differentiate
25 Metric volume measure
26 Long-handled tool
27 Short dagger
30 Aura, slangily
33 Work on the cutting edge?
34 Groovy
35 *The Dukes of Hazzard* deputy
36 Catalonia locale
37 Artist Rockwell
38 Suffix for Catholic
39 *Enterprise* officer
40 Contents of Santa's mail
41 Maine crustaceans
43 Go down swinging
44 Incompetent
45 Jeff in *True Grit*
49 Send into exile
51 Gossip
52 Collect in return
53 Shake a tail
55 Joy Adamson's cat
56 Puccini's "Vissi d'___"
57 Time in power
58 Persian Gulf missile
59 Food colorings
60 Napped
61 "___ Leaving Home": Beatles

DOWN

1 Double quartet
2 Suspect's story
3 Types
4 Soliloquies
5 Burlesque
6 Frome of fiction
7 Kill
8 Funny pair?
9 Response
10 Turn a deaf ear to
11 Mania
12 Great Plains Indians
13 Like a yenta
21 Speed Wagons
23 Beatles album
25 Small groove
27 Has the leading role
28 Smoke glass
29 ___ out (withdraws)
30 One of seven for Salome
31 ___ many words
32 Make a buzzing noise
33 Burst of energy
36 Police dog
37 Benignity
39 All-purpose trucks
40 Put down carpet
42 Wesley in *U.S. Marshals*
43 Good buddy
45 Stir slightly
46 Flash flood area
47 Follow as a consequence
48 Heaps
49 Pitt in *Moneyball*
50 Wispy
51 Pop test
54 Burnett of advertising

★★ Keep Going

Start on a blank square of your choice and connect as many blank squares as possible with one single continuous line. You can only connect squares along vertical and horizontal lines, not along diagonal lines. You must continue the connecting line up until the next obstacle, i.e., the rim of the box, a black square or a square that has already been used. You can change direction at any obstacle you meet. Each square can be used only once. The number of blank squares that will be left unused is marked in the upper square. There is more than one solution. We show only one solution.

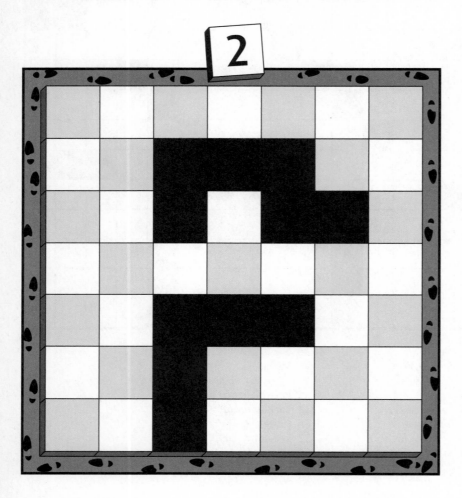

REPOSITION PREPOSITION

Unscramble DREAM IF SO and find a two-word preposition.

★ Word Ladder

Convert the word at the top of the ladder into the word at the bottom, using all the rungs in between. On each rung, you must put a valid word that has the same letters as the word above it, apart from one letter change. There may be more than one way of achieving this.

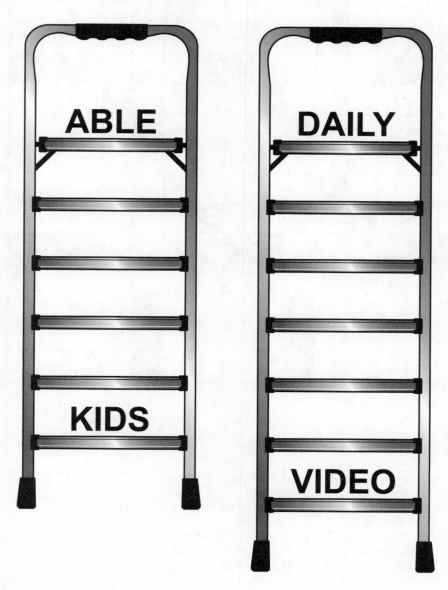

FRIENDS?

What do the following words have in common?

QUARREL FOUR AWE LONE MEDDLE LITHE

★★★★★ Celebrity Chuckles by Kelly Lynch

ACROSS

1 Classic song by the Kinks
5 Early Iranian
9 Unwanted mail
14 Gossipy twosome
15 Concluded
16 Ryan in *Barry Lyndon*
17 "Monopoly" rollers
18 "Do, ___, fa, sol ..."
19 It may make the cut
20 Hard sugar for a biting wit?
23 Poker great Phil
24 Windburned
25 Scalawag
28 Bar order
30 Chapel seat
33 Like royal jelly
34 Scrupulously avoid
35 Deep cut
36 Home to a woman of letters?
39 Joule fractions
40 Ache
41 More under the weather
42 ___ Anne de Beaupré
43 Stopping action on a ball
44 Water nymph
45 Michael Caine's title
46 Added stipulations
47 Comic's gallows jokes?
54 Of a zone
55 *Doctor Zhivago* heroine
56 "___ a Gal I Love": Sinatra
58 *Fiddler on the Roof* matchmaker
59 A party to
60 Honduras port
61 Rob of *90210*
62 Watch over
63 Succor

DOWN

1 Can cover
2 Narc ending
3 Poland's Walesa
4 2011 Presidents Cup winners
5 Bit of gossip
6 "___ Breath You Take": Sting
7 Test-drive car
8 "Flying Scotsman" Liddell
9 Wild feline
10 Not a blood relative
11 Unfatty
12 *Saigon* star Alan
13 Weaver's reed
21 The Donald's ex
22 Danish currency
25 Four-star reviews
26 Here and there?

27 Lightly burn
28 Bilbo Baggins' home
29 Jabba the ___
30 St. ___ Girl beer
31 German steel city
32 What place?
34 Bolted
35 *The Vicar of Wakefield* novelist
37 Go around and around
38 Adherent of the Vedas
43 Books from the Gideons
44 Let go
45 Oceanic ray
46 Ohio college town
47 Singer ___ P. Morgan
48 *Iliad* warmonger
49 One-___ sale
50 Settled down
51 Split rattan

52 Double curve
53 Lucky streak
57 Light knock

★★★ BrainSnack®—Automation

These inspection robots work only in pairs. Which robot (1–12) isn't needed?

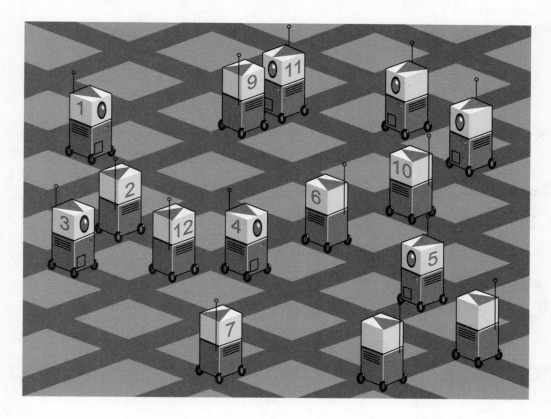

CONNECT TWO

An oxymoron is a combination of seemingly contradictory or incongruous words, such as "science fiction"(science means "knowledge or study dealing with facts or truth" while fiction means "an imagined or invented creation"). Connect the words with meanings that oppose each other and make oxymorons.

CLEARLY	MAYBE
DEFINITE	CONFUSED
FREE	SECRET
OPEN	RENT

★ Word Wheel

How many words of three or more letters, each including the letter at the center of the wheel, can you make from this diagram? No plurals or conjugations. We found 18, including one nine-letter word. Can you do better?

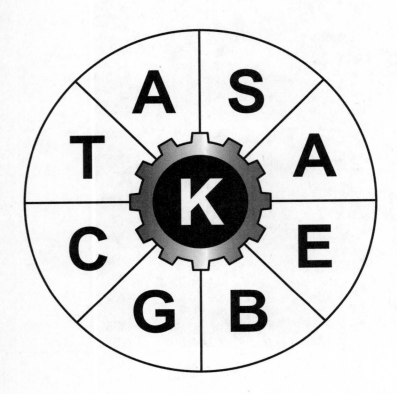

LETTER LINE

Put a letter in each of the squares below to make a word which means "SUPPORTER." The number clues refer to other words which can be made from the whole.

4 1 6 7 10 8 2 3 RELUCTANT; 10 7 6 6 6 5 1 THIN LEAF;
6 10 8 10 5 1 MONUMENT; 4 8 5 2 3 SPOOK;
8 9 9 1 2 3 AGREEMENT

1	2	3	4	5	6	7	8	9	10

★★★★★ Nobility by Peggy O'Shea

ACROSS

1 Ellipsoidal
5 Gregorian ___
10 Little League stats
14 Honduran seaport
15 Roberts of *Fawlty Towers*
16 Stallion's supper
17 Crushed underfoot
18 Really shine
19 BBC viewer
20 Did the bidding of
22 Carve in relief
24 Not so rosy
26 Alice B. Toklas' friend
27 Moderately slow tempo
30 U2 guitarist
33 Overcharge
34 Gypsy's deck
36 ___ gratia artis
37 "My Way" lyricist
38 Martin in *Bobby*
39 Spacewalks
40 Glacier substance
41 *Moonstruck* song (with "That's")
42 Israel's chief port
43 Settled snugly
45 In need of a drink
47 Oft-bitten things
48 It's yelled on Wall Street
49 Poppycock
51 Houston hoopster
55 Went on horseback
56 First track, often
60 Earthenware pot
61 State point-blank
62 From Oslo
63 Oil burner
64 Graceful water bird
65 Texas breakfast choice
66 Book of Mormon book

DOWN

1 Dr. Octavius in *Spider-Man 2*
2 Action word
3 Burn balm
4 "Poker Face" singer
5 Things are bought on it
6 Put a jinx on
7 RSA political party
8 Before marriage
9 PBS fundraiser
10 *My Three Sons* son
11 He became a Cavalier in 2011
12 "That's the Way ___": Dion
13 Concordes
21 Northern Ireland river
23 Confront
25 Approaches
26 Local map lines
27 Now and ___
28 Present purpose
29 Ebbets Field center fielder
31 Political funny business
32 History class assignment
35 ___ Lingus airline
38 ___ salts
39 *Survivor: Fiji* winner
41 Shepard's ___ *of the Mind*
42 Hawaiian city
44 Place to throw darts
46 Champions
49 "Oh, phooey!"
50 Amble
52 Ku Klux ___
53 Roper of the polls
54 Military funeral sound
57 Neither here ___ there
58 Prefix for cycle
59 Q–U links

★★★ Sport Maze

Draw the shortest way from the ball to the goal. You can only move along vertical and horizontal lines, not along diagonal lines. The figure on each square indicates the number of squares the ball must be moved in the same direction. You can change direction at each stop.

2	5	1	4	5	2
2	2	3	3	2 (ball)	2
2	4	1	2	4	4
2	4	1	2	1	2
1	2	2	2	4	1
4	1	(goal)	5	1	5

DOUBLETALK

Homophones are words that share the same pronunciation, no matter how they are spelled. If they are spelled differently then they are called heterographs. Find heterographs meaning:

HOTEL ACCOMMODATION and SUGARY

★★★ Word Sudoku

Complete the grid so that each row, each column and each 3 x 3 frame contains the nine letters from the black box below. The hidden nine-letter word is in the diagonal from top left to bottom right.

A B E F M O R S T

REPOSITION PREPOSITION

Unscramble FINO CAFE and find a three-word preposition.

★ Spot the Differences

Find the nine differences in the image on the right.

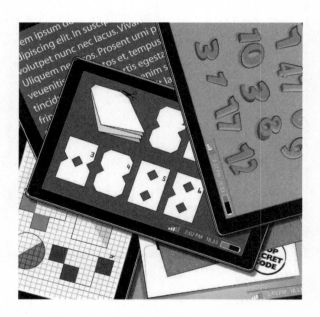

WORD SHRINKS

Make each word shorter by taking away one letter at a time but keeping the remaining letters in their original order and form a new word. Do this as many times as possible, forming a new word as each letter is deleted. Example : PLATE ➡ LATE ➡ ATE ➡ AT

STOOP

★★★★★ Themeless by Karen Peterson

ACROSS

1 Bryn ___ College
5 Impish one
10 "___ Hear Music": Beach Boys
14 Word form for "field"
15 Where James Bowie died
16 Gossip maven Barrett
17 Former Mets stadium
18 German pistol
19 Book of Mormon book
20 Like male models
22 "Dear" friend
24 Do the mall
25 "___, With Love": Lulu hit
26 Spielberg's "go"
29 Outerwear item
32 Taxi driver in *Taxi*
33 Heath shrub
34 West in *My Little Chickadee*
35 "*Dies ___*" (Requiem Mass hymn)
36 Inscribed
37 Kindle ___
38 32,000 ounces
39 Karpov's game
40 Incendiarism
41 Like Pollock's art
43 *District 9* prawns
44 Album insert
45 Greek house
46 Grade of beef
48 Doc Brown's dog
52 Cologne address
53 Phileas Fogg's creator
55 Kathryn of *Law & Order: CI*
56 Scraps of food
57 Great Lakes tribesmen
58 Sheepskin leather
59 Mosquito, e.g.
60 South African coins
61 Recovering from surgery

DOWN

1 Radar's show
2 Ottoman Empire VIP
3 House bird
4 Billboard locale
5 Judge Roy Bean's "court"
6 Grass cluster
7 Opera singer Haugland
8 M.'s partner
9 Victim of a drift net
10 Double-edged
11 Give and take
12 Kournikova of tennis
13 It gets pounded
21 "Beat it, gnat!"
23 Ye olde Anglo-Saxon serf
25 Mini-pies
26 *The Red Tent* author Diamant
27 St. John's bread
28 Conveys
29 Henhouse perch
30 Hank who hit home runs
31 They're coming of age
33 Choreographer José
36 "It doesn't matter"
37 Apple doughnuts
39 Comfy shoe
40 "What a pity!"
42 Something to quench
43 James of *Gunsmoke*
45 Penalized
46 Take an ax to
47 Roll response
48 Ireland
49 Switch attachment?
50 Structural beam
51 Leakes of *TRHoA*
54 Mesozoic, e.g.

★★★ BrainSnack®—Stained Glass

Which stained-glass window (A–D) does not belong?

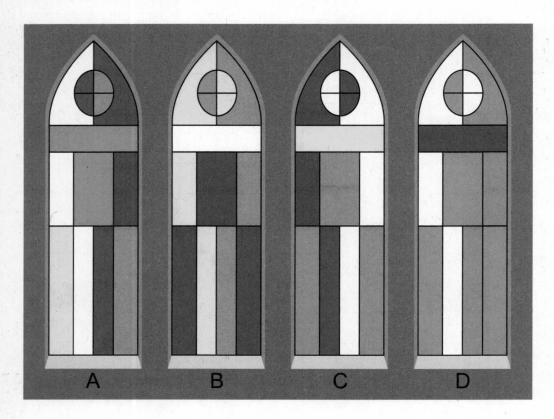

BLOCK ANAGRAM

Form the word that is described in the brackets with the letters above the grid. Extra letters are already in the right place.

OSCARS (Native American sport)

★ Collect

All the words are hidden vertically, horizontally or diagonally—in both directions. The letters that remain unused form a sentence from left to right.

```
V A L U A B L E S P A C O L S
L E C T O R A C U R T I V S H
S S E X H I B I T I O N E L E
P T L U L Y L U A D C O O A E
I K I E N S S N T E F O O R T
R R I C B I I P S T T E I E M
T M S S K A Q M M S O S O N U
S M D E G E L U H A P N O I S
C N R R E W R E E H T A S M I
I O A E S A L S N V E S W S C
M B C M I L T U P I N S E S S
O M E I S S O M N N W L Y E T
C G N T P O S T E R S E N L C
S A O S S U E R E Y F R A G E
E T H A S R S E L B R A M N J
L H P P N T H A T B U N O I B
L E T E H I N G G O M E T S O
S R T T H R O W N H S A W A Y
```

HOBBY
INTERNET
MARBLES
MINERALS
MUSEUM
OBJECTS
PASTIME
PHONE CARDS
PINS
POSTERS
PRIDE
RAGE
SELL
SHEET MUSIC
SHELLS
SINGLES
SMURFS
STAMPS
STATUS
STICKERS
SWAP
UNIQUE
VALUABLE
WINE LABELS

BARGAIN
BUTTONS

COINS
COMIC STRIPS

EXHIBITION
GATHER

SANDWICH

What five-letter word belongs between the word on the left and the word on the right, so that the first and second word, and the second and third word, each form a common compound word or phrase?

R H I N E _ _ _ _ _ W A L L

★★★★★ **MLB Mascots** by Michele Sayer

ACROSS
1 "This weighs ___!"
5 Cryptographic
10 Prig
14 Decorate freshly
15 ___ and beyond
16 Blanchett in *Notes on a Scandal*
17 Deplaned, e.g.
18 Principle
19 Plugging away
20 Ace's team
22 Take great pleasure in
24 Semiotics study
25 Silent *Duck Soup* star
26 Woman in Lennon's "Woman"
27 Isinglass
28 Rajon Rondo's org.
31 *Hannah Montana* character
34 Lou Seal's team
36 Huffington Post buyer
37 Plumber's tool
39 Throw on the floor
40 Jock's wife in *Dallas*
42 TiVo ancestor
43 Black suit
46 Land in the sea
47 University conferral
48 Chapeau carrier
49 Grey Cup stats
51 Albertville river
53 Bureaucratic bind
57 From Odense
59 Southpaw's team
60 New York cardinal
61 Exceedingly
63 Africa's longest river
64 Standout
65 Pamphleteer of 1776
66 River through central Germany
67 Miss on the brae
68 The Witch House site
69 What's remaining

DOWN
1 Fiery horses
2 British boob tube
3 Abhorrence
4 Dell product
5 L.L. Bean mailing
6 Does what a good dog does
7 Knotts and Adams
8 Garden party?
9 Divert
10 Charge a fortune
11 Screech's team
12 Williams of the Temptations
13 Sister of Meg, Jo, and Amy
21 Operatic tenor Vickers
23 Remove from the board
25 Bivalve joint

27 Norman Lear sitcom
29 Be plenty hot
30 Away from the wind
31 "Answer, please"
32 Make a small move
33 Fredbird's team
35 Ready to blow one's top
38 Selleck's *Blue Bloods* costar
41 He's all ears
44 "If you play your cards right"
45 NOW founder Gloria
50 Former insecticide
52 Nasal congestion locale
53 Bonn river
54 Stage whisper
55 Ends of the earth
56 Use energetically

57 "The Farmer in the ___"
58 Oaxaca water
59 Mimic a banshee
62 Ovine sound

★★ BrainSnack®—Pick a Side

Which view (1–5) of this castle is wrong?

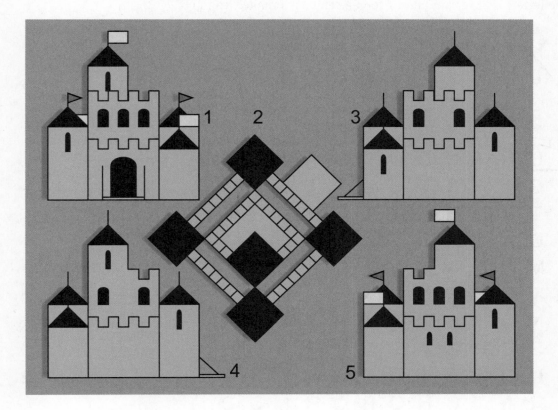

CHANGELINGS

Each of the three lines of letters below spell a word that has an occupational connection, but the letters have been mixed up. Four letters from the first word are now in the third line, four letters from the third word are in the second line and four letters from the second word are in the first line. The remaining letters are in their original places. What are the words?

U L A C R S M I K R

L N D E B T A J E C

B U M K E R T A H K

★ Hip Hop

All the words are hidden vertically, horizontally or diagonally—in both directions. The letters that remain unused form a sentence from left to right.

```
H I P K A H P I O N E E R S O
P E N L N E X T I N C E T R E
Y U M O A R T S E I C A S E R
F O B Y U E F A T R R E N P N
G U R U H T N O D F U A I P E
S C A G I R K T L U I T U A G
S S Z T R H H A I T S N L R L
S S I D A G M S S E T H A U A
N H L M M E A I N T M F E A C
A I M T G B R O N X F I E R I
B E P N G H H O W I R R N O S
R N U S C P B A T G O I N E U
U O O U O E R I M S W M I X M
L S C R A T C H O B O R L D O
R T C T H E L L A C I A M A J
I I B T R I C K Y T E E R T S
M O F E O A F T H E E C N A D
X H I P N H O P A R T I S T T
```

CULTURE
DANCE
DISS
EMINEM
EXTINCE
FUNK
GHETTO
GRAFFITI
GURU
HAMMER
JAMAICA
LOUNGE
MARIHUANA
MICROPHONE
MIX
MUSICAL GENRE
OUTKAST
PIONEERS
RAPPERS
RHYME
SCRATCH
SPIN
STARFLAM
STREET
TOAST
TRICKY
URBAN
USHER

AEROSOL CAN   BEATBOX   BRONX
AMBIENT   BRAZIL   CHRISTIAN

UNCANNY TURN

Rearrange the letters of the phrase below to form a cognate anagram, one which is related or connected in meaning to the original phrase. The answer can be one or more words.

CAN'T RELY ON IT

★★★★★ Capital Namesakes by John M. Samson

ACROSS

1 School mil. program
5 Speedway sound
10 Antiquing device
14 Aviating prefix
15 Prefix with structure
16 Pother
17 Get ___ a good thing
18 One getting stuffed
19 Corey in *The Lost Boys*
20 Ontario city*
22 Like a runway model
24 Sicilian summer resort
26 Instead of
27 Copyist
29 Indiana's "Lake City"*
32 Not true
33 With merriment
35 "By what means?"
37 Source of pollen
38 Kicks out of office
39 Are in the past?
40 Tumult
41 Desired guests
42 Chicago airport
43 Moves obliquely
45 Personify
47 Beehive state
48 Disquiet
49 Border town of northern New York*
52 Van Zandt of *The Sopranos*
56 By mouth
57 Cul-___ (dead-end street)
61 Corona
62 Zachary of *Chuck*
63 Shelley's Muse
64 Some van Goghs
65 Arabian Sea gulf
66 Get *Mad* again
67 Lea Michele series

DOWN

1 Racetrack fence
2 Wine prefix
3 2010 Disney film
4 Abbreviate
5 Washington, D.C. suburb*
6 Cytoplasm component
7 Frequently, to Byron
8 Valuable strike
9 Fugitive hunters
10 City in Georgia*
11 Hockey score
12 Polish a draft
13 Central New York city*
21 Generous offer
23 Modify
25 Misery
26 A social network
27 City in NE Texas*
28 1985 film set in Greece
30 *The Road ___*: Bill Gates
31 "What, me ___?": Alfred E. Neuman
32 Big name in bouquets
34 Jerk
36 Mini
38 Janet Fitch's *White ___*
39 All the way
41 Tenor's higher-up
42 A few last words?
44 Columbus, Ohio suburb*
46 Idaho border city*
49 *Shark Tale* dragon fish
50 Riled up
51 Lay away
53 Rockies resort
54 Blonde in *Legally Blonde*
55 Muzzle
58 Before
59 ___ Quentin
60 Suffix for emir

★★ Sudoku Twin

Fill in the grid so that each row, each column and each 3 x 3 frame contains every number from 1 to 9. A sudoku twin is two connected 9 x 9 sudokus.

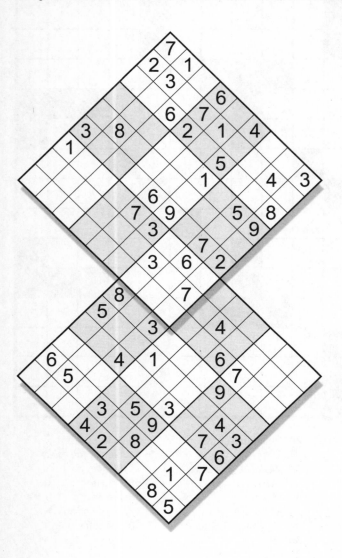

DOODLE PUZZLE

A doodle puzzle is a combination of images, letters and/or numbers that represent a word or a concept. If you cannot solve a doodle puzzle, do not look at the answer right away. Think hard—and outside the box.

★★ Keep Going

Start on a blank square of your choice and connect as many blank squares as possible with one single continuous line. You can only connect squares along vertical and horizontal lines, not along diagonal lines. You must continue the connecting line up until the next obstacle, i.e., the rim of the box, a black square or a square that has already been used. You can change direction at any obstacle you meet. Each square can be used only once. The number of blank squares that will be left unused is marked in the upper square. There is more than one solution. We show only one solution.

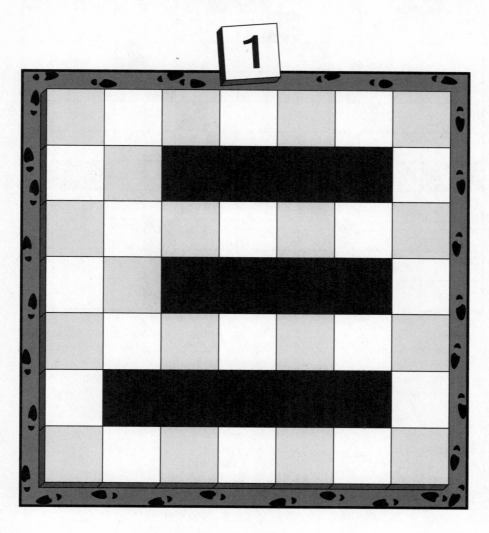

REPOSITION PREPOSITION

Unscramble POETRY OR APART and find a two-word preposition.

★★★★★ Weather-Wise by John M. Samson

ACROSS

1 Guinness in *The Detective*
5 Third-stringer
10 Dame Everage
14 Minderbinder in *Catch-22*
15 Seismograph detection
16 Necessity
17 Markedly similar
18 Incited
19 Decorative arch
20 Fan undulations at Miami NBA games?
22 Feline murmurs
23 The Old Sod
24 Former Genoese magistrate
25 Pain in the neck
28 ___ pike
32 Deep-felt
33 Worker's incentive
34 Scooby-___
35 Criminal charges
36 MLB commissioner Bud
37 Stereotypical hobo apparel
38 Paris–Lyon direction
39 Bluegrass partner of Scruggs
40 Check recipient
41 Harry Potter's friend
43 Swanson in *The Phantom*
44 Batman's hideaway
45 "Super!"
46 Sexologist Hite
48 Unfriendly facade?
53 Steersman's station
54 SE Asian capital
55 Gravelly ridges
56 Column part
57 Newark's "The Rock" is one
58 Utah ski resort
59 Like today, tomorrow
60 Jacobi in *I, Claudius*
61 Toontown judge

DOWN

1 Far East nurse
2 Relish
3 Astronomer Millosevich
4 Matches
5 Checkerboard space
6 Parabola
7 Fashion craze
8 Hula instruments
9 Lake floor
10 *The World Is Not ___* (1999)
11 Commencement times?
12 ___-do-well
13 Field drinks
21 Sly stratagem
22 Chef's equipment
24 Merck product
25 Like Siberian winters
26 "___ of do or die ..."
27 Smartphones, e.g.?
28 Nick in *Warrior*
29 "Get___!" ("Start working!")
30 Noted thesaurian
31 Meddlesome
33 Lima or pinto
36 Fruity gin flavoring
37 B&O, for one
39 Till bill
40 Faculty member
42 Rockies rodent
43 Alaskan bear
45 Dolly the sheep, e.g.
46 Boutique
47 Sister of Zeus
48 Concern
49 Rare person
50 Kon-Tiki Museum site
51 The Spanish call it OTAN
52 Streetcar
54 Taken advantage of

★ Monkey Business

Some of the older students have been monkeying about with the BEST KIDS BOOKS titles list in the library. Can you fix it?

1 DUSTIEST HERO
   by SE Hinton

2 KINGLIEST SHARP WIN
   by James Watson

3 LIMP ON KEN
   by Herve Tullet

4 PROGGED
   by Mini Grey

5 THE RAKISH PRANK
   by Nick Sharratt

6 ATHLETE RE WHO
   by Graeme Base

DOUBLETALK

Homophones are words that share the same pronunciation, no matter how they are spelled. If they are spelled differently then they are called heterographs. Find heterographs meaning:

FROM TREES and EXPRESSES DESIRE OR INTENT

★ Cats

All the words are hidden vertically, horizontally or diagonally—in both directions. The letters that remain unused form a sentence from left to right.

```
I F A C A A T E C N A L A B D
H W O E S L B S T N O T H M A
V A E C D B I Y O A N T A I A
C R I T R E S A S W I L I L T
F M R R I N S H W S L L H C F
U T I U B G I U M I I T E P A
R H A L P A H N P S D N N U N
Y Z A L K L L A R O I N I G G
T H E G P I P L F I U R P A S
T S T U I 6 0 D A Y S N S O N
S O S T A L K W F I T K C S C
O S M L C K E I H T C F E E U
L T H C L E I N I I N T C C R
I N H E A T A T T F S E N I I
T N U H W T N O T L T K L M O
A E T I B B E S O E C I E I U
R E S E M A I S A A N O L R S
Y E R P S N A R L S W I Z E D
```

FANGS
FLEAS
FUR
HAIR BALL
HISS
HUNT
IN HEAT
KITTEN
LAZY
MEOW
MICE
MILK
PAPILLA
PET
POUNCE
PREY
PURR
PUSS
SIAMESE
SILENT
SNARL
SOLITARY
SPINE
STALK
TAIL
TICKS
TOMCAT
WAIL
WARMTH
WHISKER

ABYSSINIAN
AGILE
BALANCE

BENGALI
BIRDS
BITE

CLAW
CLIMB
CURIOUS

ONE LETTER LESS OR MORE

The word on the right side contains the letters of the word on the left side plus or minus the letter in the middle. One letter is already in the right place.

G A R F I E L D (+U) ☐ ☐ ☐ ☐ G ☐ ☐ ☐ ☐

★★★★★ # The Play's the Thing by John M. Samson

ACROSS

1 CBS eye, e.g.
5 Colorful lizard
10 Doctor of afternoon TV
14 Color similar to flax
15 Silky synthetic
16 Ward in *Almost Golden*
17 "In a cowslip's bell I lie." play
19 Phillips University city
20 Latticework
21 Battened down
23 Suffering from dementia
24 Macbeth or Gaga
25 Unless, in law
27 "Mellow Yellow" singer
30 Sees eye to eye
33 Faucet issues
35 Wall Street newbie: Abbr.
36 Minstrel songs
37 Society's finest
38 Skewbald
39 Hurler's pride
40 Bread spreads
41 Nullifies
42 Lexicographer Noah
44 Leap ___
46 Cast-of-thousands film
47 When tulips bloom
51 Actress Flockhart
54 Impassive
55 Classical Roman poet
56 "My kingdom for a horse!" play
58 Christmas tree
59 Dimwit
60 Neuter a horse
61 "... happily ___ after."
62 Hindu social class
63 Limerick language

DOWN

1 Riga natives
2 Earth tone
3 Shrek's color
4 Preliminary sketches
5 Mailer's ___ *of the Night*
6 Fissures
7 Popeye's assent
8 Trunk growth
9 Gazelle
10 Fake
11 "Press not a falling man too far!" play
12 "Should ___, madam?": Shak.
13 Alan in *Shane*
18 Couturier Perry
22 Recyclable items
26 Wastrel
27 Lightheaded
28 Parodied
29 "Yes" signals
30 Nitpicker's find
31 Swiss waterway
32 "Hath Britain all the sun that shines?" play
34 Brazil cruise stop
37 Like the Tesla Roadster
38 What Goldilocks ate
40 Driftwood in *A Night at the Opera*
41 Contrail
43 Miss Muffet's scarer
45 Big house
48 Slicker
49 They grow on you
50 Ride the updrafts
51 Manage all right
52 Tel ___
53 Verdi opera
54 Scotch measure
57 ___ *for Corpse*: Grafton

★★★ Sunny Weather

Where will the sun shine? With the knowledge that each arrow points to a place where a symbol should be, can you locate the sunny spots? The symbols cannot be next to each other vertically, horizontally or diagonally. A symbol cannot be placed on top of an arrow. We show one symbol.

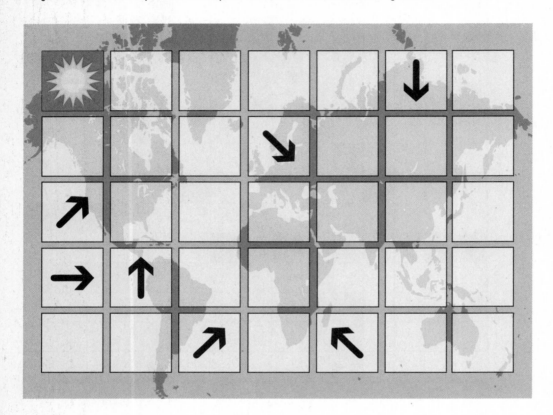

UNCANNY TURN

Rearrange the letters of the phrase below to form a cognate anagram, one which is related or connected in meaning to the original phrase. The answer can be one or more words.

TERM OF SUCH HATE

★★★ Concentration—Letter Division

Draw three straight lines from side to side so that five sections are created, each one containing the first five letters of the alphabet.

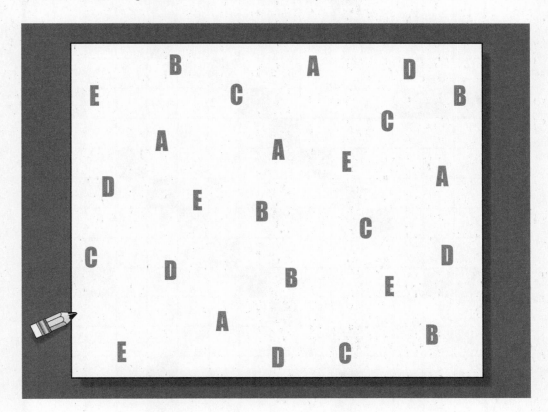

END GAME

The words you are seeking all have the letters END in them in the position indicated. When you have found all of the answers, from the clues on the right, one column will reveal the END GAME word which can tighten.

_	_	_	_	E	N	D	Holds up fiction
E	N	D	_	_	_	_	And finally...
_	_	_	E	N	D	_	Stories handed down
_	E	N	D	_	_	_	Caring for

_ _ _ _ E N D   Holds up fiction
Ē N D _ _ _ _   And finally...
_ _ _ Ē N D _   Stories handed down
_ Ē N D _ _ _   Caring for

★★★★★ Big Words II by John M. Samson

ACROSS

1 Inform the host
5 Full
10 Pronto!·
14 Mimic
15 Florida *CSI* setting
16 ___ San Lucas
17 Having large feet
19 The yoke's on them
20 Flapjacks
21 Pauline's problems
23 Evened the score
24 Retired French coin
25 Jog the memory
28 Flourishes
31 Belch
32 Desire
33 Back muscle, briefly
34 Floor decor
35 Pontificate
36 Kind of chest
37 Caesar's 250
38 Salty imperative
39 Abdul or Cole
40 Glabrous
42 Filmed
43 Clockwork, mostly
44 Byron or Tennyson
45 Vampire repellent
47 Cajole
51 His, to Henri
52 The symbol #
54 Plunders
55 Eurasian elk
56 Substance
57 Geoffrey of *Shine*
58 Caught morays
59 *Enchanted* Hathaway role

DOWN

1 Coarse file
2 Pet welfare org.
3 Band of gold
4 It makes perfect
5 Like Virginia ham
6 Lent support to
7 New Mexico tourist town
8 Five-foot-tall bird
9 Refute
10 Squirrel's stash
11 Growing among rocks
12 First fratricide victim
13 Coloratura Lily
18 Primer, for one
22 Make bearable
24 Lester of bluegrass
25 Gag
26 Durance of *Smallville*
27 Ill temper

28 Military leaders
29 Syrup source
30 Lieu
32 Crude
35 Defeat
36 Like Apollo
38 Half a Basque game
39 W Australia capital
41 Enjoy with gusto
42 Hit high
44 Freewheeling
45 Teri in *Oh, God!*
46 Baseball brothers
47 Plane for limited runways
48 City on the Oka River
49 "C'mon, be ___!"
50 Animal-rights org.
53 Track rival of Ovett

★★ The Puzzled Librarian

The new library assistant accidentally bumped into the Good Reads notice board, and the magnetic letters all fell off. The librarian remembered the authors' names, but needs some help to get the titles right, as the chief librarian will be back in ten minutes!

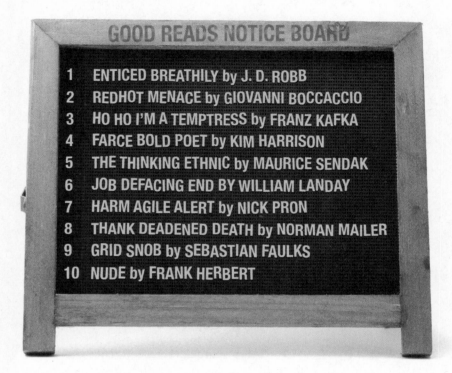

GOOD READS NOTICE BOARD

1   ENTICED BREATHILY by J. D. ROBB
2   REDHOT MENACE by GIOVANNI BOCCACCIO
3   HO HO I'M A TEMPTRESS by FRANZ KAFKA
4   FARCE BOLD POET by KIM HARRISON
5   THE THINKING ETHNIC by MAURICE SENDAK
6   JOB DEFACING END BY WILLIAM LANDAY
7   HARM AGILE ALERT by NICK PRON
8   THANK DEADENED DEATH by NORMAN MAILER
9   GRID SNOB by SEBASTIAN FAULKS
10 NUDE by FRANK HERBERT

SANDWICH

What five-letter word belongs between the word on the left and the word on the right, so that the first and second word, and the second and third word, each form a common compound word or phrase?

SHOE _ _ _ _ _ OUT

★ Guitarists

All the words are hidden vertically, horizontally or diagonally—in both directions. The letters that remain unused form a sentence from left to right.

```
R E L F P O N K B A R R E T T
T B T H O M P S O N H S E F R
L A E M T D R A H N I E R Y O
L E N N O N B O Y A N G T L L
T O W N S H E N D J H O L L Y
A R Y M Z O E R S O I V C E A
R A E N B A N J R H I I M B T
U I L K L H P E E N N A D D R
O I I X O E I P T S E S G A E
M N A E C O R A A O L R L E Y
L C B N K O H N W N S I O L D
I E I R E D O N C L A P T O N
G R E D O O C B Y N E H T E M
P N A H G U A V E E E O I F Y
T H I E B E S T G C L U F R I
S A C K S I O N I T K R R A R
P E T T Y I R O S S I E A S T
S E S N I L L O C V B E P M R
```

CLAPTON
COLLINS
COODER
GILMOUR
HOLLY
HOOKER
JOHNSON
KING
KNOPFLER
LEADBELLY
LENNON
MARLEY
METHENY
MOORE
PARFITT
PETTY
PRINCE
REINHARDT
ROSSI
SACKSIONI
SEGOVIA
TAYLOR
THOMPSON
TOWNSHEND
VAUGHAN
WATERS
ZAPPA

BAILEY
BARRETT

BECK
BENSON

BERRY
BLOCK

WORD SHRINKS

Make each word shorter by taking away one letter at a time but keeping the remaining letters in their original order and form a new word. Do this as many times as possible, forming a new word as each letter is deleted. Example : PLATE ➡ LATE ➡ ATE ➡ AT

FORUM

★ Futoshiki

Fill in the 5 x 5 grid with the numbers from 1 to 5 once per row and column, while following the greater than/lesser than symbols shown. There is only one valid solution that can be reached through logic and clear thinking alone!

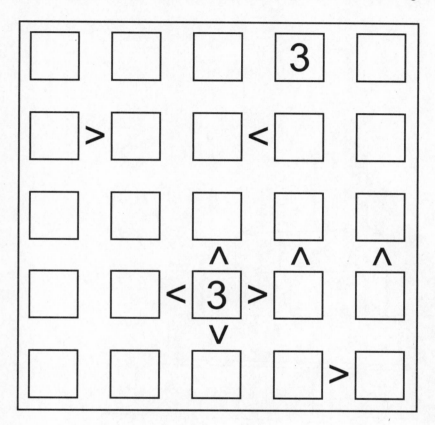

LETTER LINE

Put a letter in each of the squares below to make a word which means "REPLACEMENT." The number clues refer to other words which can be made from the whole.

1 2 6 7 10 1 HOTEL ROOMS; 4 2 3 4 10 9 UNIT;
9 8 3 10 1 CYLINDRICAL PASSAGEWAYS;
7 8 9 2 1 DANCEWEAR; 3 2 4 5 BROKE

1	2	3	4	5	6	7	8	9	10

★ Word Pyramid

Each word in the pyramid has the letters of the word above it, plus a new letter.

M
(1) before noon
(2) human limb
(3) planet
(4) wise
(5) academic degree
(6) composer
(7) toward a water source

ONE LETTER LESS OR MORE

The word on the right side contains the letters of the word on the left side plus or minus the letter in the middle. One letter is already in the right place.

L E A R N I N G (+G) ☐ N ☐ ☐ ☐ ☐ ☐ ☐ ☐

★★★ BrainSnack®—Red or Green

Which square (A–L) is the wrong color?

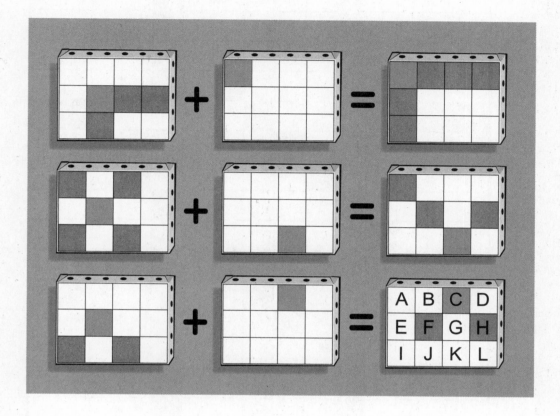

BLOCK ANAGRAM

Form the words that are described in the brackets with the letters above the grid. Extra letters are already in the right place.

KITESURFING (dancing on ice)

		G						A			

★★★★★ Big Words III by John M. Samson

ACROSS

1 "God" singer Tori
5 Ebenezer's partner
10 Frizzy coif
14 "Along ___ a spider ..."
15 New Mexico county
16 2001 Johnny Depp film
17 Spendthrift
19 David's father-in-law
20 Record holder?
21 Ratifies
23 Coastal eagles
24 Edgar Bergen dummy
25 Industrialist DuPont (1771–1834)
28 Colors in mists
31 Brand of breath mints
32 Creator of Sam-I-Am
33 Squeaky wheel's need
34 000 in letters
35 Slanting
36 Scandinavian epic
37 "Yang Yang" singer Yoko
38 Sandalwood, e.g.
39 Roman physician
40 Supplants
42 Feel indignation
43 Steamy
44 40-day pre-Easter period
45 Expressing anguish
47 One meaning of -ish
51 Paella pot
52 Writing desk
54 Cubist Mondrian
55 Draws close to
56 *Garfield* pooch
57 Loosen
58 Makes unferal
59 "Houston" singer Martin

DOWN

1 "High Voltage" band
2 Picasso's Dora
3 Prefix meaning "all"
4 Divisions
5 Woodward in *Rachel, Rachel*
6 Mountains of NW Africa
7 Convent room
8 Limonite, e.g.
9 Plant scientist
10 Take in fully
11 Nonsense
12 Drubbing
13 Barn birds
18 Current lines
22 Iniquity locales
24 ___ Sainte Marie
25 Blood of the gods
26 See former classmates
27 They love to work
28 Rider's handful
29 Enlarge
30 Diagonal
32 Warhorse
35 Chance happening
36 *Changeling* director
38 Identical
39 *The Balcony* playwright
41 Crescent-shaped
42 Careless
44 Peter in *Beat the Devil*
45 St. Peter's Square VIP
46 Et ___ (and others)
47 Flimflam
48 Conceal
49 Renée Fleming solo
50 MTV viewer, often
53 Bounding main

PAGE 15

First-Name Basis

N	I	P	A		T	A	N	G	O		A	B	U	T
E	L	U	L		I	L	I	A	D		L	O	R	I
W	I	L	L	Y	N	I	L	L	Y		T	B	A	R
T	A	P	I	O	C	A	S		S	T	A	B	L	E
			N	U	T	S		U	S	U	R	Y		
M	A	J	O	R	S		O	P	E	N		S	O	B
E	T	O	N	S		F	R	E	Y	A		O	S	E
O	R	H	E		R	E	I	N	S		I	C	O	N
W	I	N		S	I	T	E	D		A	N	K	L	E
S	A	N		O	P	A	L		R	U	S	S	E	T
		Y	O	Y	O	S		P	E	R	T			
C	O	C	O	A	S		F	O	L	I	A	T	E	S
U	T	A	H		T	E	R	R	Y	C	L	O	T	H
B	I	K	E		E	R	A	T	O		L	I	N	E
A	C	E	D		S	E	T	O	N		S	L	A	P

PAGE 16

Number Cluster

CONNECT TWO

BONELESS RIBS, ALL ALONE, LONG SHORTS, FIRM ESTIMATE

PAGE 17

BrainSnack®—Tennis

Letters

J. Place all the letters next to each other. They make up a logical series in which two letters are always skipped. A-bc-D-ef-G-hi-J-kl-M, etc.

DOUBLETALK

ANT/AUNT

PAGE 18

Gigi

C	H	O	P		S	T	A	L	E		O	G	L	E
R	E	M	O		P	A	C	E	R		B	R	A	D
A	R	O	W		A	T	R	I	A		T	E	T	E
G	O	O	D	G	R	I	E	F		P	A	T	E	N
	E	O	S			A	R	I	A					
D	E	G	R	E	E	S		A	M	O	N	G	S	T
A	L	O	E	S		E	U	R	O	S		A	T	E
W	I	L	D		S	T	A	L	K		F	R	E	E
N	O	D		S	T	O	W	E		S	A	B	I	N
S	T	E	T	S	O	N		N	A	T	I	O	N	S
	N	I	T	A			N	A	T					
P	A	G	E	S		G	R	E	Y	G	H	O	S	T
U	L	A	R		B	E	A	N	O		F	L	E	E
N	A	T	E		O	N	I	O	N		U	L	N	A
T	I	E	D		S	E	N	S	E		L	A	D	S

PAGE 19

Sauces

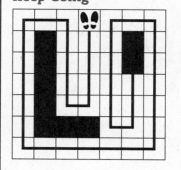

A sauce is a substance that is prepared separately, makes a dish easier to digest and gives extra flavor.

FRIENDS?

Each can have the prefix OVER- to form a new word.

PAGE 20

Keep Going

UNCANNY TURN

FAMILY TREE

PAGE 21

Women Writers

A	R	M	S		O	P	R	A	H		A	J	A	R
B	E	E	T		D	O	O	N	E		N	A	P	E
E	D	N	A	F	E	R	B	E	R		E	N	O	L
T	O	U	R	I	S	T	S		C	O	M	E	D	Y
			T	O	S	S		C	U	R	I	A		
R	E	G	I	N	A		M	O	L	E	C	U	L	E
E	L	E	N	A		W	I	N	E	S		S	I	X
A	L	O	G		S	I	N	G	S		S	T	A	T
M	I	R		H	E	D	D	A		S	E	E	N	O
S	E	G	M	E	N	T	S		V	E	R	N	A	L
			E	A	R	T	H		S	E	R	E		
L	E	S	S	E	E		P	E	T	U	N	I	A	S
A	D	A	H		N	G	A	I	O	M	A	R	S	H
S	I	N	E		C	R	A	Z	E		D	O	T	E
T	E	D	S		E	R	R	E	D		E	N	I	D

PAGE 22

Sudoku

4	7	9	8	1	3	5	6	2
3	5	6	9	4	2	8	7	1
2	8	1	7	6	5	4	9	3
6	9	3	2	5	1	7	4	8
1	4	8	3	7	9	2	5	6
5	2	7	6	8	4	1	3	9
8	3	4	1	9	7	6	2	5
9	1	5	4	2	6	3	8	7
7	6	2	5	3	8	9	1	4

SANDWICH

AGE

PAGE 23

Sport Maze

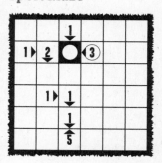

CHANGE ONE, CHANGE ANOTHER

SEAT ➡ HEAT ➡ MEAT ➡ MELT

PAGE 24
How Sweet It Is!

A	B	B	A		C	L	A	S	P		R	S	V	P
P	E	E	P		H	E	L	L	O		A	W	O	L
E	A	R	P		E	M	A	I	L		T	E	L	A
S	U	G	A	R	L	A	N	D		S	T	E	E	N
			R	U	S	T			E	L	A	T		
S	C	H	E	M	E		G	R	E	E	N	B	A	Y
A	R	O	N			A	S	L	E	E	P		A	L	A
Y	E	N	T	L		T	E	N		T	O	S	I	R
S	E	E		A	D	O	N	I	S		B	I	N	D
O	L	Y	M	P	I	A	N		A	I	S	L	E	S
			R	A	S	E		A	D	I	T			
C	L	Y	D	E		J	O	H	N	C	A	N	D	Y
L	A	D	D		R	A	R	E	E		C	I	A	O
A	L	E	E		I	N	C	A	S		L	A	N	G
D	O	R	N		B	E	A	D	S		E	S	A	I

PAGE 25
Word Sudoku

R	A	Q	T	N	I	E	O	S
O	E	N	S	R	Q	T	A	I
I	T	S	E	O	A	N	Q	R
Q	O	R	I	A	E	S	T	N
T	N	I	R	S	O	Q	E	A
A	S	E	N	Q	T	I	R	O
N	Q	T	O	I	R	A	S	E
E	I	O	A	T	S	R	N	Q
S	R	A	Q	E	N	O	I	T

DELETE ONE

Delete S and find PALMISTRY.

PAGE 26
BrainSnack®—Row Your Boat

5 people. Four oarsmen and a coxswain. You can discover this because there is not an extra oar visible at the front of the top image.

CONNECT TWO

GLOBAL VILLAGE, ALMOST PREGNANT, FORGOTTEN MEMORIES, LOUD WHISPER

PAGE 27
Alley Talk

B	A	R	D		O	M	A	R	S		S	A	L	T
A	S	O	R		C	O	L	I	C		A	L	I	I
S	T	R	I	K	E	U	P	T	H	E	B	A	N	D
S	O	Y	B	E	A	N	S		O	N	R	I	C	E
			E	N	T			C	O	C	A			
B	L	I	M	P	S		N	O	N	I	S	S	U	E
E	A	S	E			S	O	R	E	N		P	T	L
S	P	L	I	T	T	H	E	P	R	O	F	I	T	S
O	S	A		S	H	I	N	S			B	R	E	E
T	E	M	P	E	R	E	D		C	R	I	E	R	S
			E	T	E	S		T	O	O				
E	S	P	O	S	A		C	H	A	M	P	I	O	N
S	P	A	R	E	D	N	O	E	X	P	E	N	S	E
M	A	N	I		E	E	R	I	E		C	O	L	A
E	T	T	A		D	O	E	R	R		K	N	O	T

PAGE 28
Binairo

0	0	1	1	0	0	1	1	0	1	1	0
0	0	1	0	1	1	0	0	1	1	0	1
1	1	0	0	1	0	0	1	1	0	0	1
0	0	1	1	0	1	1	0	0	1	1	0
1	1	0	0	1	0	1	0	1	0	1	0
1	0	0	1	1	0	0	1	0	1	0	1
0	0	1	1	0	1	0	1	1	0	0	1
0	1	1	0	0	1	1	0	1	0	1	0
1	1	0	0	1	0	1	1	0	1	0	0
1	0	0	1	0	1	0	0	1	0	1	1
0	1	1	0	0	1	1	0	0	1	0	1
1	1	0	1	1	0	0	1	0	0	1	0

LETTER LINE

BENEFICIAL: FELINE; NIECE; FABLE; FENCE; CABIN

PAGE 29
Spot the Differences

BLOCK ANAGRAM

HUNTING

PAGE 30
Sporting Joes

A	C	L	U		S	T	R	U	T		P	R	E	Y
R	O	I	L		T	H	E	S	E		R	E	D	S
I	C	E	T		R	A	D	A	R		I	N	G	E
L	O	U	I	S	A	N	D	F	R	A	Z	I	E	R
			M	C	I			A	G	E				
O	B	T	A	I	N	S		A	P	O	S	T	L	E
H	A	R	T			N	A	D	I	R		H	E	T
G	R	E	E	N	E	A	N	D	N	A	M	A	T	H
O	R	A		A	N	G	I	E			O	N	T	O
D	E	T	E	C	T	S		R	E	P	R	E	S	S
			A	R	R			L	A	P				
T	O	R	R	E	A	N	D	N	U	X	H	A	L	L
O	R	A	N		N	A	I	A	D		E	L	I	A
F	E	T	E		C	R	E	P	E		U	T	E	P
U	S	E	D		E	A	S	E	D		S	A	N	D

PAGE 31
Cage the Animals

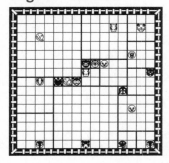

DOUBLETALK

NONE/NUN

PAGE 32
Tools

A bench vise is an aid that secures items while working on them.

DELETE ONE

Delete E and find COMPENSATION.

PAGE 33

Sunny Weather

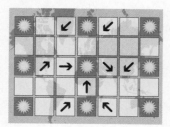

UNCANNY TURN
CONFESSIONAL

PAGE 34

There's Something About...

C	A	P	P		D	W	E	E	B		A	D	A	M
A	R	A	L		W	A	I	V	E		R	I	S	E
L	E	I	A		A	I	R	E	S		I	O	W	A
M	A	R	Y	T	Y	L	E	R	M	O	O	R	E	
			G	I	N			I	R	S				
B	E	C	O	M	E	S		O	R	T	O	L	A	N
O	B	I	E			C	O	U	C	H		A	M	O
M	E	R	R	Y	M	O	N	T	H	O	F	M	A	Y
B	R	R		O	A	R	E	D			L	A	T	E
S	T	I	C	K	I	N		O	S	M	O	S	I	S
		E	E	N			T	A	U					
	W	I	L	L	Y	O	U	M	A	R	R	Y	M	E
H	I	D	E		A	L	L	O	T		I	M	A	N
I	T	E	R		R	E	A	V	E		S	C	A	D
S	H	A	Y		D	A	R	E	D		H	A	M	S

PAGE 35

Kakuro

8	5	6			6	2	1
1	2			2	8	1	
7	4	2		9			
			3	8	2	4	
3		1	4		7		
1	6	7			2	3	5
6	7			6	1	9	

DELETE ONE
Delete D and find CORRUPTION.

PAGE 36

BrainSnack®—Winner

12. The number after the decimal point is half of the number before the decimal point. 24.12.

CHANGELINGS

F O O T L I G H T S
U N D E R S T U D Y
P E R F O R M I N G

PAGE 37

Presidential Nicknames

W	I	N	K		T	R	O	T		S	T	E	L	E
O	N	E	I		H	E	R	O		A	R	I	E	L
J	O	H	N	T	Y	L	E	R		N	I	S	E	I
O	R	I	G	A	M	I		R	E	D	N	E	S	S
			D	R	E	C	K		L	A	I	N		
G	I	J	O	E	S		A	B	E	L		H	A	T
A	D	A	M	S		F	R	O	G	S		O	B	I
R	A	M	S		D	I	A	R	Y		S	W	A	M
T	H	E		T	E	N	O	N		P	I	E	C	E
H	O	S		O	I	N	K		M	A	D	R	A	S
	K	R	I	S		E	L	I	D	E				
D	E	P	A	L	M	A		I	S	R	A	E	L	I
A	D	O	R	E		J	E	F	F	E	R	S	O	N
I	N	L	E	T		A	N	T	I		M	A	R	K
S	A	K	E	S		R	E	S	T		S	U	D	S

PAGE 38

Keep Going

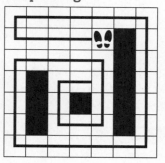

REPOSITION PREPOSITION
WITH REFERENCE TO

PAGE 39

Sudoku

2	6	7	9	1	8	5	3	4
1	5	4	7	3	6	2	9	8
9	8	3	2	5	4	6	7	1
4	9	2	8	7	5	1	6	3
3	1	5	4	6	9	8	2	7
8	7	6	1	2	3	4	5	9
6	3	9	5	8	1	7	4	2
5	2	8	3	4	7	9	1	6
7	4	1	6	9	2	3	8	5

ONE LETTER LESS OR MORE
BOREDOM

PAGE 40

Diana's Realm

B	I	R	D		C	L	A	M	P		F	E	A	T
A	M	O	I		L	E	C	A	R		A	R	C	O
H	A	L	F	M	O	O	N	C	O	O	K	I	E	S
S	T	E	F	A	N	I	E		C	R	E	E	D	S
			I	B	E	X		S	E	E	R			
S	P	A	D	E	D		S	U	E	S		A	P	E
H	O	V	E	L		A	C	I	D		U	L	A	R
M	O	O	N	L	I	G	H	T	S	O	N	A	T	A
O	N	I	T		N	A	M	E		R	A	N	T	S
O	A	R		A	F	R	O		L	A	S	S	I	E
			A	R	E	S		B	A	C	H			
S	O	C	C	E	R		O	U	T	L	A	S	T	S
T	H	E	M	A	N	I	N	T	H	E	M	O	O	N
A	I	D	E		A	R	E	T	E		E	U	R	O
G	O	E	S		L	A	S	E	R		D	R	E	W

PAGE 41

Futoshiki

3	1	2	4	5
5	3 < 4	2	1
1 < 2	5	3	4
4	5	3	1 < 2
2	4 > 1	5 > 3

DOODLE PUZZLE
SunSpots

PAGE 42

Word Sudoku

T	F	V	R	U	O	N	A	L
O	A	N	F	V	L	T	R	U
U	L	R	N	T	A	F	O	V
V	N	O	A	R	F	L	U	T
L	R	T	V	N	U	A	F	O
F	U	A	L	O	T	V	N	R
A	T	L	O	F	R	U	V	N
R	V	U	T	A	N	O	L	F
N	O	F	U	L	V	R	T	A

LETTERBLOCKS

LEGGING
SANDALS

PAGE 43

BrainSnack®—Home Port

A. Read as follows: the second and second last letter of the previous port are the first and last letter of the next port.

DOUBLETALK

LESSEN/LESSON

PAGE 44

36 Across

PAGE 45

Cage the Animals

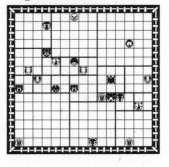

FRIENDS?

Each can add the prefix OUT- to form a new word.

PAGE 46

Binairo

0	I	0	I	I	0	0	I	0	I	I
I	0	I	I	0	I	0	0	I	I	0
0	I	I	0	I	0	I	0	I	0	I
I	0	0	I	I	0	0	I	0	I	I
I	I	0	I	0	I	I	0	I	0	0
0	I	I	0	I	0	I	I	0	I	0
I	0	I	0	I	I	0	I	0	0	I
0	I	0	I	0	I	I	0	I	I	0
I	0	0	I	I	0	I	I	0	I	0
0	I	I	0	0	I	0	I	I	0	I
I	0	I	0	0	I	I	0	I	0	I

CONNECT TWO

ANXIOUS PATIENT, JUMBO SHRIMP, LIGHT SHADE, AUTO PILOT

PAGE 47

Chairman of the Board

P	A	I	R		C	A	B	E	R		W	A	I	F
O	N	C	E		A	G	I	L	E		A	N	T	I
W	I	T	C	H	C	R	A	F	T		I	G	E	T
E	M	U	L	A	T	E	S		U	T	T	E	R	S
R	E	S	I	D	U	E		G	R	U	E	L		
			N	O	S		C	O	N	C	R	E	T	E
O	F	T	E	N		D	E	R	E	K		Y	E	N
L	A	H	R		C	O	D	E	D		F	E	N	D
O	V	A		R	O	W	A	N		L	A	S	T	S
R	E	T	A	I	L	E	R		D	A	D			
			S	T	O	O	L		L	O	V	E	S	T	O
P	I	L	O	T	S		M	A	N	E	A	T	E	R
O	L	I	N		S	U	M	M	E	R	W	I	N	D
S	A	F	E		A	N	D	I	E		A	N	T	E
E	Y	E	D		L	U	C	A	S		Y	G	O	R

PAGE 48

BrainSnack®—Snakeskin

1. The skin's color pattern consists of black alternated with a colored square. The piece of snakeskin on a yellow background gets the same color as the background.

SANDWICH

WORD

PAGE 49

Actions

Every type of action means something to the person performing the act and it can be designated as understandable behavior.

UNCANNY TURN

GRAND FINALE

PAGE 50

1950s No. 1 Hits

M	E	N	U		B	A	L	L	S		I	B	A	R
I	V	A	N		E	L	I	O	T		M	Y	T	H
M	A	Y	B	E	L	L	E	N	E		P	E	L	E
I	N	S	I	S	T	E	D		A	R	A	B	I	A
			A	T	E	N		E	M	E	R	Y		
H	I	S	S	E	D		F	R	I	T	T	E	R	S
A	N	T	E	S		C	L	I	N	E		L	I	T
S	C	A	D		S	L	A	N	G		V	O	L	E
T	A	G		T	H	A	T	S		C	O	V	E	N
A	N	G	R	I	E	S	T		T	O	L	E	D	O
		E	A	R	L	S		R	O	T	C			
F	E	R	R	E	T		C	A	P	T	A	I	N	S
I	L	L	E		E	A	R	T	H	A	N	G	E	L
G	A	E	L		R	A	I	S	A		I	O	N	E
S	L	E	Y		S	A	B	O	T		C	R	E	W

PAGE 51

BrainSnack®—Choose Your Cheese

Cheese cube 3. The mouse chooses the cheese cubes with the fewest number of holes. It already collected the cubes with 0, 1, 2 and 3 holes. The cube with four holes is the next one.

DELETE ONE

Delete T and find SINGAPORE.

PAGE 52

Sudoku

4	9	1	8	6	2	7	5	3
2	3	7	9	5	4	6	1	8
8	5	6	1	7	3	4	9	2
5	8	9	2	1	6	3	4	7
7	2	4	3	9	8	5	6	1
1	6	3	5	4	7	8	2	9
3	1	8	4	2	5	9	7	6
9	7	5	6	8	1	2	3	4
6	4	2	7	3	9	1	8	5

END GAME

A M E N D E D
E N D U R E R
V E N D U E S
E N D E M I C

PAGE 53

1960s No. 1 Hits

PAGE 54

Word Sudoku

G	R	A	U	M	S	T	D	I
S	U	D	I	R	T	M	G	A
M	T	I	G	D	A	R	U	S
A	G	M	T	U	D	S	I	R
I	S	R	M	A	G	U	T	D
U	D	T	S	I	R	G	A	M
T	A	U	D	S	M	I	R	G
R	M	G	A	T	I	D	S	U
D	I	S	R	G	U	A	M	T

BLOCK ANAGRAM

MOUNTAIN CLIMBING

PAGE 55

Sport Maze

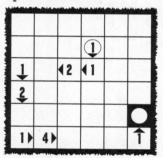

DELETE ONE

Delete S and find SAHARA DESERT.

PAGE 56

1970s No. 1 Hits

PAGE 57

BrainSnack®—Name That Dessert

TIRASUMI. The last syllable, SU, is always swapped with the successive syllables of the first word, so TI is swapped first, then RA and then MI.

DOUBLETALK

BROACH/BROOCH

PAGE 58

Sudoku Twin

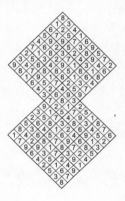

DOODLE PUZZLE

FeedBack

PAGE 59

1980s No. 1 Hits

PAGE 60

Sunny Weather

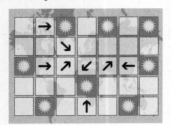

DELETE ONE

Delete S and find ADDITION.

PAGE 61

BrainSnack®—Olives

Group 5. Each group consists of three types of olives. The sum of two types is always equal to the quantity of olives of the third type.

SANDWICH

COPY

PAGE 62

Safe Code

$$21 \rightarrow 42 \rightarrow 84$$
$$\downarrow \ \times 2$$
$$336 \leftarrow 168$$

LETTERBLOCKS

ASPIRIN
SURGERY

PAGE 63

Beer Belly

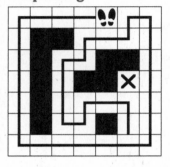

PAGE 64

Hourglass

(1) skyline, (2) silken,
(3) links, (4) sink, (5) knit,
(6) stink, (7) thinks,
(8) knights

LETTERBLOCKS

STABLE
TRACTOR

PAGE 65

Keep Going

DELETE ONE

Delete S and find CHANDELIER.

PAGE 66

Diminutive

PAGE 67

BrainSnack®—Red Letter

Letter G. All letters next to a vowel are red.

CONNECT TWO

BAD LUCK, CIVIL DISOBEDIENCE, EVEN ODDS, HOUSE BOAT

PAGE 68

Electro Technology

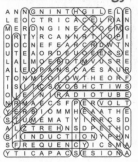

An electrical engineer can refer to resources and theories from mathematics and physics.

WORD SHRINKS

STAND ➡ SAND ➡ AND ➡ AN

PAGE 69

Open Winners (Tennis)

PAGE 70

Number Cluster

DOUBLETALK

THRONE/THROWN

PAGE 71

BrainSnack®—City Break

4—Kaapstad. Every other letter is written backward in all the other cities. The D was not written backward in Kaapstad.

FRIENDS?

Each can add the suffix -HOOD to form a new word.

PAGE 72

Open Winners (Golf)

B	O	S	C		S	U	M	A	C		P	A	N	E
A	M	A	H		P	L	U	T	O		A	L	E	A
R	I	T	A		R	A	M	O	N		E	A	R	S
S	T	E	L	L	A	R		M	C	I	L	R	O	Y
		M	A	N			E	L	L					
T	H	E	E	D	G	E		C	R	E	A	M	E	R
W	O	R	R	Y		M	E	H	T	A		E	D	O
I	W	A	S		H	E	L	L	O		E	L	I	A
R	I	T		T	O	N	I	O		F	R	E	T	S
L	E	O	N	A	R	D		E	A	R	N	E	S	T
		R	R			S	E	I						
A	N	D	R	O	I	D		S	H	E	E	H	A	N
B	E	A	M		B	R	U	N	O		E	A	V	E
A	N	T	A		L	A	S	E	R		L	A	O	S
S	E	A	N		E	M	C	E	E		S	S	N	S

PAGE 73

Sport Maze

2▶	4▶	◀1	◀3		5▼
			③▼		
					○
			▲4		
					▲3

LETTER LINE

STRAWBERRY: BARTERS; BREWS; STARRY; STRAW; WEARS

PAGE 74

Word Sudoku

T	O	S	E	A	M	L	P	F
F	E	P	S	O	L	A	M	T
A	L	M	T	P	F	S	O	E
M	F	L	P	E	T	O	S	A
O	A	T	M	L	S	E	F	P
P	S	E	O	F	A	M	T	L
L	P	O	F	S	E	T	A	M
S	T	A	L	M	P	F	E	O
E	M	F	A	T	O	P	L	S

BLOCK ANAGRAM

MARTIAL ART

PAGE 75

Best Supporting Actors

M	E	N	A		A	L	O	N	E		A	T	E	E
A	W	O	L		S	I	T	O	N		P	I	L	L
R	E	D	B	U	T	T	O	N	S		I	M	A	M
C	R	E	A	T	U	R	E		H	E	A	R	T	S
		C	I	T	E		U	R	A	N	O			
C	A	J	O	L	E		A	S	I	S		B	A	S
O	H	A	R	E		B	L	U	N	T		B	S	A
M	A	C	E		M	O	O	R	E		M	I	T	T
I	R	K		M	I	X	U	P		H	E	N	R	I
C	D	L		U	S	E	D		D	A	N	S	O	N
		E	D	I	T	S		P	O	S	T			
C	A	M	E	R	A		C	U	R	T	A	I	N	S
L	I	M	N		K	A	R	L	M	A	L	D	E	N
A	R	O	N		E	R	A	S	E		L	E	I	A
D	E	N	Y		S	A	B	E	R		Y	E	L	P

PAGE 76

Sudoku

4	5	9	7	3	8	2	1	6
6	8	2	5	4	1	7	3	9
3	7	1	9	6	2	8	5	4
2	1	5	8	7	4	6	9	3
8	9	6	1	2	3	4	7	5
7	3	4	6	5	9	1	8	2
5	2	3	4	1	7	9	6	8
9	6	7	2	8	5	3	4	1
1	4	8	3	9	6	5	2	7

SANDWICH

COACH

PAGE 77

BrainSnack®—Missing Cube

Cube 8. The number in a circle equals the sum of the red cubes minus the sum of the blue cubes.

CHANGE ONE, CHANGE ANOTHER

SONG ➡ SONS ➡ TONS ➡ TOES

PAGE 78

Best Supporting Actresses

O	N	A	N		S	T	O	A	T		P	A	S	T
A	C	T	A		L	I	N	G	O		E	N	N	A
T	A	T	U	M	O	N	E	A	L		S	N	I	P
S	A	U	S	A	G	E	S		E	S	T	A	T	E
		E	V	A	S		C	R	I	S	P			
R	E	M	A	I	N		R	E	A	P		A	C	E
O	D	E	T	S		J	O	L	T	S		Q	E	D
W	I	L	E		S	U	S	I	E		S	U	N	G
A	N	I		S	T	R	I	A		R	A	I	S	E
N	A	S		A	R	O	N		D	O	N	N	E	D
		S	E	V	E	R		S	E	A	T			
F	L	A	X	E	N		S	I	L	L	I	E	S	T
L	I	L	I		G	E	E	N	A	D	A	V	I	S
I	D	E	S		T	R	A	C	Y		G	I	L	A
T	O	O	T		H	A	L	E	S		O	L	O	R

PAGE 79

Spot the Differences

END GAME

E N D O W E D
E N D P L A Y
F E N D E R S
E N D W I S E

PAGE 80

Horoscope

REPOSITION PREPOSITION

TOGETHER WITH

PAGE 81

Futoshiki

3	1	2	4	5
2	3 < 4	5	1
1 < 2	5	3	4
5 > 4 > 1	2	3
4	5	3	1 < 2

LETTERBLOCKS

ANATOMY
HABITAT

PAGE 82

Famous Arians

O	L	A	N		I	N	T	E	L		O	G	E	E
L	I	M	O		S	E	I	N	E		R	E	A	R
L	E	O	N	A	R	D	O	D	A	V	I	N	C	I
A	U	R	O	R	A			L	E	T	H	E		
			L	E	W		S	T	A	N				
R	A	V	I	O	L	I		P	O	S	T	M	E	N
O	M	I	T			T	R	I	N	I		O	L	A
P	O	P	E	B	E	N	E	D	I	C	T	X	V	I
E	R	E		A	D	E	L	E			R	I	E	L
S	T	R	A	N	D	S		R	A	P	I	E	R	S
			R	A	Y	S		S	R	O				
S	I	T	O	N					T	R	O	O	P	S
T	H	O	M	A	S	J	E	F	F	E	R	S	O	N
L	A	M	A		A	A	R	A	U		A	S	E	A
O	D	E	S		G	N	A	R	L		L	A	M	P

PAGE 83

Antiques

More recent work such as Jugendstil and Art Deco is also considered to be antique.

DOUBLETALK

AISLE/ISLE

PAGE 84

Sunny Weather

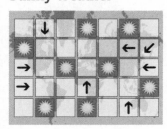

ONE LETTER LESS OR MORE

CLEANED

PAGE 85

Famous Leos

H	I	T	S		B	E	S	O	M		S	L	R	S
A	S	A	P		E	A	R	L	E		T	O	I	L
D	A	N	I	E	L	R	A	D	C	L	I	F	F	E
J	O	A	N	N	A		H	E	F	T	E	D		
			S	C	I	S		B	A	A	L			
D	A	K	T	A	R	I		A	N	N	E	A	L	S
E	P	E	E	S		P	A	P	I			M	A	I
A	L	F	R	E	D	H	I	T	C	H	C	O	C	K
L	E	I			R	O	N	I		E	A	R	T	H
S	A	R	A	Z	E	N		S	T	E	R	E	O	S
			C	O	N	S		T	A	L	I			
S	T	A	T	I	C			V	E	L	D	T	S	
W	I	L	T	C	H	A	M	B	E	R	L	A	I	N
A	R	O	W		E	D	G	A	R		O	M	N	I
M	E	T	O		D	E	M	O	N		N	E	A	T

PAGE 86

BrainSnack®—Current Account

1569. The following calculations are always performed with the two first numbers: $3 - 2 = 1$, $3 + 2 = 5$, $3 \times 2 = 6$, $3^2 = 9$.

CONNECT TWO

HALF FULL, INVISIBLE INK, ILL HEALTH, OLD BOY

PAGE 87

Kakuro

1	4	5		6		5	9	8
3	8		1	3	8		6	3
5	2	1	7		9	7		6
7		9	6	2		8	9	5
2	7	4	3		9	5	8	
	6		8	2	5		5	3
9	2	8		3	8	4		9
3		5	8	1		1	3	8
8	3	9	1		2	9	5	7

UNCANNY TURN

MOTHER COUNTRY

PAGE 88

Famous Sagittarians

A	C	H	E		A	R	E	N	A		B	R	O	M
H	O	E	S		D	U	R	E	R		A	I	D	E
E	D	W	A	R	D	G	R	O	B	I	N	S	O	N
M	A	N	U	A	L			O	S	I	E	R	S	
			V	E	T		E	R	O	S				
T	B	I	L	I	S	I		N	E	P	H	E	W	S
H	O	S	E			M	A	C	A	O		V	I	I
E	R	S	K	I	N	E	C	A	L	D	W	E	L	L
T	E	E		N	O	S	E	S			A	R	C	O
A	R	I	A	D	N	E		E	M	B	R	Y	O	S
			D	I	E	S		D	U	E				
S	H	R	U	G	S				T	A	I	C	H	I
T	O	U	L	O	U	S	E	L	A	U	T	R	E	C
O	B	I	T		C	H	E	A	T		C	E	R	E
P	O	N	S		H	E	N	C	E		H	E	E	D

PAGE 89

Word Sudoku

F	D	G	M	N	I	O	V	R
M	O	I	V	F	R	D	G	N
N	V	R	D	O	G	M	I	F
I	N	F	G	D	O	R	M	V
V	R	M	F	I	N	G	O	D
D	G	O	R	M	V	N	F	I
G	F	V	N	R	M	I	D	O
R	I	D	O	G	F	V	N	M
O	M	N	I	V	D	F	R	G

SANDWICH

BALL

PAGE 90

Keep Going

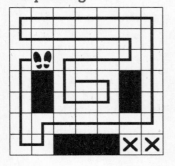

REPOSITION PREPOSITION

ACCORDING TO

PAGE 91

Tee for Two

T	I	F	F		S	H	A	P	E		U	T	E	S
A	L	O	U		H	E	L	I	X		N	U	D	E
R	I	A	L		E	L	E	C	T		E	M	I	L
T	A	L	L	T	A	L	E		E	N	A	M	E	L
			P	E	T			R	O	S	Y			
A	T	T	A	C	H	E		T	I	N	Y	T	O	T
D	O	U	G	H		A	C	H	O	O		U	W	E
M	O	R	E		B	R	I	A	R		U	C	L	A
I	N	K		M	U	L	A	N		A	S	K	E	R
T	E	E	T	I	M	E		A	M	N	E	S	T	Y
			Y	A	K	S			A	I	D			
A	N	T	L	E	R		T	U	R	N	T	A	I	L
D	I	R	E		U	L	E	N	T		O	L	G	A
A	N	O	N		S	E	E	D	Y		B	O	O	N
M	A	T	T		H	O	N	O	R		E	T	T	A

PAGE 92

Sport Maze

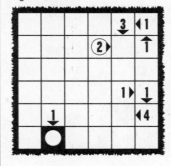

LETTERBLOCKS

FORWARD
REBOUND

PAGE 93

Sudoku

1	9	7	8	2	5	3	6	4
4	8	6	1	3	7	9	5	2
3	2	5	9	6	4	7	8	1
8	7	2	3	4	1	6	9	5
5	3	9	2	8	6	1	4	7
6	4	1	7	5	9	8	2	3
7	1	8	4	9	2	5	3	6
9	5	4	6	1	3	2	7	8
2	6	3	5	7	8	4	1	9

DOODLE PUZZLE

ReadY

PAGE 94

BrainSnack®—Game On

Video game machine 3. The black squares should be green.

BLOCK ANAGRAM

SNOWBOARDING

PAGE 95

Themeless

PAGE 96

New York

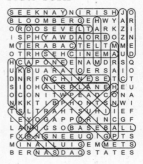

New York is home to the headquarters of the United Nations, with the flapping flags of its member states.

DOUBLETALK

GROAN/GROWN

PAGE 97

BrainSnack®—Switch Around

Switch 1. Each switch rotates 90° per column. In the odd columns (1 & 3) they rotate counterclockwise and in the even columns (2 & 4) clockwise.

ONE LETTER LESS OR MORE

CANNIBALS

PAGE 98

Eastwood Films

S	E	E	P		I	N	A	P	T		A	D	A	R
A	C	T	I		R	E	N	E	W		N	I	L	E
G	R	A	N	T	O	R	I	N	O		D	R	O	P
S	U	S	P	E	N	D	S		T	O	R	T	E	S
			O	N	E	S		M	I	L	E	Y		
A	C	H	I	E	R		S	O	M	E	W	H	A	T
G	R	A	N	T		S	I	R	E	N		A	V	E
A	I	N	T		S	I	D	E	D		B	R	A	E
M	E	G		D	O	L	L	S		S	E	R	I	N
A	D	E	Q	U	A	T	E		S	P	R	Y	L	Y
		M	U	M	P	S		S	A	R	A			
S	A	H	I	B	S		A	T	T	I	T	U	D	E
O	D	I	N		U	N	F	O	R	G	I	V	E	N
D	O	G	S		D	U	R	R	A		N	E	E	D
A	S	H	Y		S	T	O	M	P		G	A	P	S

PAGE 99

Sudoku X

3	7	9	1	4	6	8	5	2
5	4	6	2	9	8	1	7	3
8	1	2	7	3	5	9	4	6
1	8	7	9	5	3	2	6	4
2	3	4	6	8	1	5	9	7
9	6	5	4	2	7	3	8	1
4	2	1	5	7	9	6	3	8
7	5	3	8	6	2	4	1	9
6	9	8	3	1	4	7	2	5

FRIENDS?

Each can add the suffix -SHIP to form a new word.

PAGE 100

Binairo

0	0	I	0	I	I	0	0	I	0	I	I
0	I	I	0	0	I	I	0	I	0	0	I
I	I	0	I	I	0	0	I	0	I	0	0
I	0	I	I	0	I	0	0	I	0	I	0
0	0	I	0	I	0	I	I	0	0	I	I
0	I	0	I	0	I	I	0	I	I	0	0
I	0	0	I	I	0	0	I	I	0	I	0
I	0	I	0	0	I	I	0	0	I	0	I
0	I	0	0	I	0	I	0	I	I	0	I
0	0	I	I	0	I	0	0	I	0	I	I
I	I	0	0	I	0	0	I	0	I	0	I
I	I	0	I	0	0	I	I	0	I	0	0

UNCANNY TURN

FASTENS A HORSE

PAGE 101

Vegan Special

S	W	I	N	G		C	A	F	E		E	F	T	S
A	E	S	I	R		O	P	A	L		S	U	R	E
P	E	A	S	O	U	P	E	R	S		K	L	E	E
			O	S	E		M	A	R	I	L	Y	N	
A	L	C	O	V	E			E	M	O				
L	I	O	N	E	S	S		T	W	O	O	F	U	S
I	N	R	E	D		A	L	O	E	S		B	R	A
G	E	N	A		T	W	I	N	S		M	E	A	L
H	A	H		S	E	E	D	Y		L	I	A	N	A
T	R	U	S	T	E	D		S	T	E	R	N	U	M
		S	K	A			A	G	A	S	S	I		
B	I	K	I	N	I	S		T	R	I				
O	D	E	R		P	O	T	A	T	O	H	E	A	D
P	E	R	T		S	A	I	L		N	O	N	C	E
P	A	S	S		O	P	E	C		S	T	E	E	L

REPOSITION PREPOSITION

CONTRARY TO

PAGE 102

Keep Going

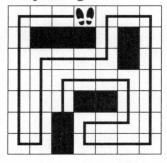

PAGE 103

BrainSnack®—Energy

Nuclei 2 and 3 are equal because A = B therefore blue = 2 x red + 1 x yellow. So 2 = 2 x (2 x red + 1 x yellow) + purple. So 3 = 2 x (2 x red + 1 x yellow) + purple.

SANDWICH

LIGHT

PAGE 104

Name That Beatles Tune!

Z	A	R	F		A	B	Y	S	M		A	S	A	P
E	C	H	O		M	A	O	R	I		N	O	N	O
S	T	I	R		P	A	N	I	C		A	M	O	K
T	U	N	N	E	L			H	E	L	E	N	E	
S	P	O	O	N	E	R		B	E	G	O	T		
			O	D	R	A		A	L	I	G	H	T	S
I	S	B	N	S		P	U	R	L	S		I	R	E
D	O	L	E		M	I	L	N	E		S	N	I	T
E	R	A		P	I	N	T	O		M	A	G	M	A
S	E	C	T	I	L	E		W	R	E	N			
		K	O	O	K	S		L	E	T	I	T	B	E
A	L	B	A	N	Y			N	A	T	I	O	N	
L	E	I	S		W	O	M	A	N		A	N	N	E
T	A	R	T		A	R	O	S	E		T	E	E	M
O	D	D	S		Y	E	A	S	T		E	D	D	Y

PAGE 105

Sport Maze

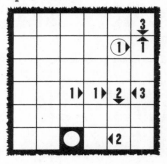

LETTERBLOCKS

GLASSES
PIANIST

PAGE 106

Sudoku X

9	5	7	4	6	2	3	8	1
3	8	4	5	1	7	9	2	6
6	1	2	9	8	3	7	4	5
8	6	3	7	2	4	5	1	9
2	4	9	1	3	5	8	6	7
1	7	5	8	9	6	4	3	2
4	3	6	2	5	9	1	7	8
7	9	1	6	4	8	2	5	3
5	2	8	3	7	1	6	9	4

CONNECT TWO

BAGGY TIGHTS, CANNED FRESH, INITIAL RESULTS, PRETTY UGLY

PAGE 107
Presidential Losers

H	E	R	B		C	R	O	P		S	A	G	E	S
E	L	I	A		O	I	S	E		I	S	E	R	E
A	L	F	L	A	N	D	O	N		S	T	R	I	A
P	E	E	L	I	N	G		D	E	T	R	A	C	T
			O	S	I	E	R		M	E	A	L		
C	A	J	O	L	E		E	V	E	R	Y	D	A	Y
A	L	O	N	E		S	P	I	E	S		F	R	O
R	A	H	S		S	K	I	E	R		S	O	A	K
L	M	N		S	P	I	N	S		S	E	R	G	E
S	O	M	E	T	I	M	E		M	A	N	D	E	L
	C	L	A	N		D	O	O	R	S				
L	O	C	A	T	E	D		P	R	A	I	R	I	E
I	R	A	T	E		A	A	R	O	N	B	U	R	R
A	R	I	E	L		T	E	A	S		L	I	E	N
M	A	N	D	Y		A	C	H	E		E	N	D	O

PAGE 108
BrainSnack®—Chime the Bells

Bell Bomnbimn. All the other bells have an i-sound and then an o-sound.

LETTER LINE

MASTERMIND: AMENDS; MADMEN; STAMMER; STRAND; SMARTEN

PAGE 109
Word Pyramid

(1) dm, (2) dim, (3) maid, (4) media, (5) diadem, (6) admired, (7) disarmed

WORD SHRINKS

WAIST ➡ WAIT ➡ WIT ➡ IT

PAGE 110
Sunny Weather

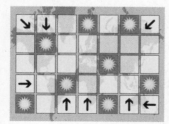

DOUBLETALK

CLAUSE/CLAWS

PAGE 111
Themeless

E	L	S	A		T	O	T	E	D		R	I	D	S
L	I	O	N		R	A	I	S	A		O	N	E	A
W	A	L	T	D	I	S	N	E	Y		C	A	L	L
E	N	T	I	R	E	T	Y		B	A	K	U	L	A
S	A	I	L	O	R	S		A	R	M	E	D		
			L	P	S		C	L	E	A	R	I	N	G
T	A	P	E	S		O	R	G	A	N		B	E	E
A	L	A	S		C	R	E	E	K		C	L	A	N
R	O	M		S	O	B	E	R		B	R	E	T	T
O	U	T	S	T	R	I	P		M	A	E			
			I	N	E	R	T		S	A	N	D	A	L	S
S	A	L	A	M	I		S	E	N	T	I	N	E	L
T	A	L	K		D	I	M	I	N	U	T	I	V	E
A	R	I	E		O	N	O	N	E		O	T	O	E
B	E	S	S		R	O	G	E	R		R	A	N	K

PAGE 112
Sudoku Twin

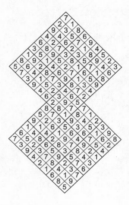

LETTERBLOCKS

BIOMASS
COMPOST

PAGE 113
Futoshiki

1	5	2	4	3
2	3	5	1	4
4	1	3 > 2	5
3 < 4	1	5	2
5	2 < 4	3 > 1

ONE LETTER LESS OR MORE

DECADES

PAGE 114
Born on Christmas Day

B	A	B	E		P	A	N	I	C		E	M	I	L
A	L	E	X		A	G	A	M	A		A	A	R	P
B	L	A	H		P	U	R	I	M		R	Y	A	N
S	I	R	I	S	A	A	C	N	E	W	T	O	N	
			B	O	Y			R	A	H				
A	D	M	I	R	A	L		S	O	D	A	P	O	P
T	R	I	T	T		L	A	L	O		R	I	A	
B	A	R	B	A	R	A	M	A	N	D	R	E	L	L
A	G	O		A	M	E	N		R	E	T	E	S	
T	O	S	C	A	N	A		G	R	A	N	A	R	Y
			A	R	C		I	C	E					
H	U	M	P	H	R	E	Y	B	O	G	A	R	T	
T	A	R	P		E	E	N	I	E		A	S	O	U
R	A	G	E		R	E	N	N	Y		D	E	A	R
Y	S	E	R		O	F	A	G	E		E	A	R	N

PAGE 115
BrainSnack®—Ghost Invader

Ghost 3. The eyes are shown in reverse on the tombstones of all the other ghosts.

BLOCK ANAGRAM

WRESTLING

PAGE 116
Concentration—Translation

2—First $((2 \times 2 \times 2)/2)/4 = 1$ and then $1/(1/2)=2$

CHANGELINGS

ANTIBIOTIC
QUARANTINE
DEPRESSION

PAGE 117
Sue Grafton's Alphabet I

PAGE 118
Keep Going

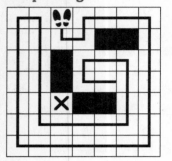

UNCANNY TURN
CONFITURE

PAGE 119
Fire Department

The fire department has a hierarchic structure to ensure smooth cooperation with, amongst others, the police.

SANDWICH
BOARD

PAGE 120
Sue Grafton's Alphabet II

C	A	M	P		A	H	E	A	D		B	E	S	T
A	R	E	A		S	I	D	L	E		A	L	L	Y
N	A	I	L		S	N	I	F	F		C	L	A	P
I	N	N	O	C	E	N	T		E	S	K	I	M	O
			A	R	T	Y		S	N	E	E			
S	C	A	L	E	S		U	N	D	E	R	T	O	W
M	A	T	T	E		P	R	E	E	N		E	S	A
A	G	I	O		E	A	G	E	R		S	E	A	L
R	E	M		U	N	S	E	R		L	U	N	G	E
T	R	E	S	P	A	S	S		R	A	I	S	E	S
			L	I	M	E		M	I	L	T			
G	U	G	I	N	O		R	I	C	O	C	H	E	T
E	N	I	D		R	O	A	C	H		A	I	D	A
L	A	N	E		E	N	U	R	E		S	L	E	D
T	S	A	R		D	E	L	O	S		E	T	N	A

PAGE 121
Sport Maze

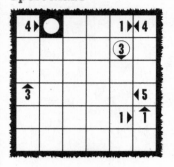

DOODLE PUZZLE
StripTease

PAGE 122
Sue Grafton's Alphabet III

A	D	A	M		M	E	T	E	S		K	O	B	E
L	E	N	A		O	L	I	V	E		I	G	O	R
A	B	I	G		S	L	E	E	P		L	E	A	R
S	I	L	E	N	C	E		L	A	W	L	E	S	S
		L	E	O	N	A		R	A	E				
O	U	T	L	A	W		C	H	A	I	R	M	A	N
B	R	I	A	R		T	R	I	T	T		O	N	O
E	G	A	N		M	O	O	R	E		S	O	T	O
L	E	R		N	I	O	B	E		W	A	L	E	S
I	S	A	B	E	L	L	A		P	H	R	A	S	E
		O	W	L		T	A	L	I	A				
B	R	E	A	T	H	E		G	U	M	S	H	O	E
L	O	W	S		O	L	M	O	S		O	E	N	O
A	B	E	T		N	A	C	R	E		T	W	I	N
H	E	R	S		E	L	I	A	S		A	N	T	S

PAGE 123
Spot the Differences

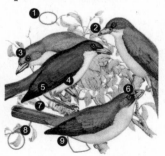

DOUBLETALK
FLAIR/FLARE

PAGE 124
Sudoku

5	2	9	6	1	3	8	7	4
3	8	7	9	4	2	6	1	5
1	6	4	8	7	5	3	2	9
6	1	5	4	8	7	2	9	3
9	4	2	3	5	6	7	8	1
7	3	8	2	9	1	5	4	6
8	7	3	1	6	9	4	5	2
4	9	6	5	2	8	1	3	7
2	5	1	7	3	4	9	6	8

LETTERBLOCKS
SKIMMER
SPATULA

PAGE 125
Word Sudoku

R	Z	U	C	X	S	O	Y	E
X	E	C	Z	Y	O	S	U	R
Y	O	S	U	R	E	X	Z	C
E	R	Y	O	S	C	Z	X	U
O	C	Z	E	U	X	R	S	Y
S	U	X	Y	Z	R	E	C	O
Z	Y	O	S	E	U	C	R	X
C	S	R	X	O	Y	U	E	Z
U	X	E	R	C	Z	Y	O	S

FRIENDS?
Each can add the suffix –WARE to form a new word.

PAGE 126
BrainSnack®—Masquerade

Color 5. Every fourth triangle is red.

CONNECT TWO
CALCULATED RISK, COUNTLESS NUMBERS, MUTE SOUND, BIG BABY

PAGE 127

Pretty Fishy

L	A	P	P			S	T	R	O	P			S	P	A	M
I	D	E	A			P	R	A	D	A			A	I	D	E
B	A	S	S	P	L	A	Y	E	R			T	K	O	S
E	G	O	T	R	I	P	S			T	E	R	E	S	A
L	E	S	I	O	N	S			D	I	V	A	S		
			M	U	T			R	E	C	A	P	P	E	D
A	R	C	E	D			K	I	L	L	S			E	L	I
L	A	O	S			A	N	N	I	E			P	A	I	N
A	G	S			O	N	E	G	A			P	I	K	A	S
N	U	M	E	R	A	L	S			K	E	N			
		I	M	A	L	L			G	A	R	N	I	S	H
N	I	C	E	L	Y			B	A	N	D	A	N	N	A
Y	A	R	N			S	E	E	R	S	U	C	K	E	R
E	G	A	D			I	N	T	R	A			L	E	A	R
T	O	Y	S			S	T	A	Y	S			E	D	D	Y

PAGE 128

Hourglass

(1) alcoves, (2) vocals,
(3) salvo, (4) oval, (5) love,
(6) olive, (7) violet, (8) violent

SANDWICH
ONE

PAGE 129

Horoscope

UNCANNY TURN
SLITHERED

PAGE 130

Themeless

P	O	E	M			H	U	M	A	N			S	T	E	P
E	L	S	A			O	T	A	R	U			O	R	L	E
L	E	A	N			N	A	H	U	M			R	O	S	E
L	O	U	T	I	S	H			M	E	D	D	L	E	R
			A	A	H				R	A	I	L			
S	T	E	R	N	U	M			M	A	N	D	E	L	A
T	E	X	A	S			A	D	E	L	E			Y	E	N
E	S	P	Y			C	O	O	L	S			N	C	O	S
A	L	E			F	O	R	G	O			D	I	A	N	E
M	A	R	T	I	N	I			N	E	U	T	R	A	L
		I	S	A	T				M	E	R			
C	H	E	E	T	A	H			A	B	S	O	L	V	E
R	U	N	T			C	A	R	L	O			G	O	A	D
A	R	C	S			T	R	E	E	S			E	L	I	N
G	L	E	E			S	I	X	E	S			N	A	N	A

PAGE 131

Opera

A rock opera like *Tommy* by The Who is a musical production with rock music in the form of an opera.

REPOSITION PREPOSITION
FORWARD OF

PAGE 132

Binairo

I	O	I	I	O	I	O	I	O	O	I
O	I	I	O	O	I	O	I	I	O	I
I	O	O	I	I	O	I	O	I	O	I
O	I	I	O	I	I	O	I	O	I	O
I	I	O	I	O	O	I	O	I	O	I
O	O	I	I	O	I	I	O	I	I	O
O	I	O	I	I	O	I	I	O	I	O
I	O	I	O	O	I	I	O	O	I	I
O	I	I	O	I	O	O	I	I	O	I
I	I	O	I	I	O	I	O	O	I	O
I	O	O	I	O	I	I	O	I	I	O

ONE LETTER LESS OR MORE
FISHING

PAGE 133

Punny Business

L	O	A	F			I	B	A	R			A	S	P	E	N
E	L	M	O			M	U	L	E			L	I	L	L	E
A	L	O	U			P	R	I	M			S	T	A	L	L
F	A	I	R	F	A	R	E			S	O	C	I	A	L
			T	A	C	O			A	K	R	O	N			
A	S	S	E	R	T			C	R	E	A	M	P	I	E
N	E	W	E	R			L	O	R	E	N			L	S	D
T	I	E	N			P	I	N	O	T			V	A	L	E
I	K	E			S	I	N	E	W			L	I	N	E	N
C	O	T	T	A	G	E	S			M	O	T	E	T	S
		S	O	N	G	S			D	A	D	A			
S	T	U	R	D	Y			M	A	D	E	M	A	I	D
L	O	I	R	E			W	O	R	D			I	T	T	O
A	F	T	E	R			H	A	L	E			N	E	S	T
G	U	E	S	S			O	N	A	N			S	E	A	S

PAGE 134

Sport Maze

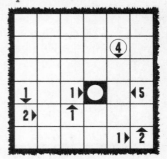

BLOCK ANAGRAM
BICYCLE RACING

PAGE 135

Kakuro

4	5	2			1	3	5			7
8			5	4	7	6			9	5
		3	7	8			7	2	1	8
5	2	6				9	6			9
6			8	4	2			1	2	3
9	1			2	6	7		7		
		5	1				6		1	8
9	3	8	6	2			9	5		
3	2			2	1			4	3	2

DOODLE PUZZLE
EinSTEIN

PAGE 136

Themeless

C	A	L	F			W	O	R	L	D			D	O	L	T
O	V	A	L			H	A	U	E	R			E	V	O	E
R	E	B	A			I	S	E	R	E			B	E	A	N
P	R	O	M	O	T	E	D			A	L	A	R	M	S
S	T	R	I	D	E	S			O	D	E	T	S		
		N	A	N			W	C	F	I	E	L	D	S
L	E	G	G	Y			L	O	T	U	S			E	E	E
A	R	O	O			F	E	R	A	L			R	E	N	T
N	I	L			D	R	E	D	D			D	E	P	T	H
A	N	D	R	O	I	D	S			F	O	P			
		W	A	N	E	S			M	I	R	A	C	L	E
H	E	A	V	E	N			B	O	N	F	I	R	E	S
A	N	T	I			D	R	O	N	E			R	E	P	S
A	T	E	N			L	I	S	T	S			E	P	E	E
S	E	R	E			Y	A	C	H	T			D	E	R	N

PAGE 137

BrainSnack®—Target Practice

Target 4. In the second outer circle the blue and purple areas that touch each other should be swapped.

DOUBLETALK

WEEK/WEAK

PAGE 138

Word Sudoku

S	P	D	L	U	R	Y	I	E
I	U	E	S	Y	D	L	R	P
Y	L	R	I	P	E	D	S	U
E	R	U	P	L	S	I	D	Y
P	D	I	U	R	Y	E	L	S
L	S	Y	E	D	I	U	P	R
D	I	P	R	E	U	S	Y	L
U	Y	L	D	S	P	R	E	I
R	E	S	Y	I	L	P	U	D

ONE LETTER LESS OR MORE

MISPLACED

PAGE 139

BrainSnack®—Windy Hill

On hill D. If you count the contour lines, you'll discover that all the other windmills are located on the 7th contour line.

UNCANNY TURN

STEAMINESS

PAGE 140

Themeless

A	R	M	S		P	L	U	M	B		S	K	I	P
L	O	O	T		L	A	N	A	I		L	A	V	E
O	L	L	A		E	N	D	O	W		O	L	A	N
F	L	A	M	E	N	C	O		E	D	W	A	R	D
T	E	R	M	I	T	E		R	E	A	L	M		
			E	R	Y		S	U	K	I	Y	A	K	I
W	E	A	R	E		C	U	R	L	S		Z	E	D
I	S	I	S		F	O	R	A	Y		S	O	R	E
N	P	R		T	R	I	L	L		M	O	O	N	S
S	Y	M	P	H	O	N	Y		V	I	C			
		A	L	A	N	S		A	E	R	A	T	E	S
O	R	I	E	N	T		P	E	N	E	L	O	P	E
M	I	L	A		I	N	E	R	T		L	I	S	I
A	C	E	S		E	E	R	I	E		E	T	O	N
N	O	D	E		R	A	T	E	D		D	Y	N	E

PAGE 141

Sudoku X

1	9	3	5	4	8	6	7	2
8	6	2	1	7	9	4	3	5
7	4	5	2	6	3	8	9	1
5	7	8	4	3	6	2	1	9
2	3	4	8	9	1	5	6	7
6	1	9	7	5	2	3	4	8
9	2	1	3	8	4	7	5	6
3	5	6	9	2	7	1	8	4
4	8	7	6	1	5	9	2	3

SANDWICH

BANK

PAGE 142

Safe Code

6 2 4 | 3 5 9
4 2 6 | 9 5 3

CHANGE ONE, CHANGE ANOTHER

FORK ➡ FORE ➡ FIRE ➡ FINE

PAGE 143

Big Words I

O	A	K	S		S	E	D	E	R		I	C	O	N
C	L	I	P		A	T	O	N	E		G	A	T	O
T	I	N	E		T	H	I	S	A		N	C	O	S
A	B	D	E	R	I	A	N		C	H	O	O	S	Y
D	I	S	C	E	R	N		S	T	E	R	E		
			H	O	E		S	T	I	L	E	T	T	O
V	I	B	E	S		S	T	R	O	P		H	I	P
E	N	O	S		S	P	A	I	N		K	E	N	T
I	S	M		U	H	U	R	A		L	I	S	T	S
L	O	B	S	T	E	R	S		F	A	N			
	I	N	E	P	T		B	R	I	D	G	E	S	
B	A	N	I	S	H		Q	U	I	D	N	U	N	C
R	E	A	P		E	L	U	D	E		E	L	S	A
A	R	T	E		R	E	I	G	N		S	C	U	D
D	Y	E	S		D	O	Z	E	D		S	H	E	S

PAGE 144

Keep Going

REPOSITION PREPOSITION

ASIDE FROM

PAGE 145

Word Ladder

able, lake, cake, deck, desk, kids;
daily, valid, alive, ideal, devil, olive, video

FRIENDS?

Each can add the suffix -SOME to form a new word.

PAGE 146

Celebrity Chuckles

L	O	L	A		M	E	D	E		B	I	L	L	S
I	T	E	M		O	V	E	R		O	N	E	A	L
D	I	C	E		R	E	M	I		B	L	A	D	E
	C	H	R	I	S	R	O	C	K	C	A	N	D	Y
		I	V	E	Y		R	A	W					
R	A	S	C	A	L		S	H	O	T		P	E	W
A	P	I	A	N		S	H	U	N		G	A	S	H
V	A	N	N	A	W	H	I	T	E	H	O	U	S	E
E	R	G	S		H	U	R	T		I	L	L	E	R
S	T	E		B	I	T	E		U	N	D	I	N	E
			S	I	R		A	N	D	S				
J	A	C	K	B	L	A	C	K	H	U	M	O	R	
A	R	E	A	L		L	A	R	A		I	G	O	T
Y	E	N	T	E		I	N	O	N		T	E	L	A
E	S	T	E	S		T	E	N	D		H	E	L	P

PAGE 147

BrainSnack®—Automation

No. 10. Two inspection robots are always looking at each other.

CONNECT TWO

CLEARLY CONFUSED, DEFINITE MAYBE, FREE RENT, OPEN SECRET

PAGE 148

Word Wheel

ask, back, bake, bask, beak, cake, sack, take, task, teak, skate, stack, stake, steak, basket, casket, backseat, backstage

LETTER LINE

ENTHUSIAST: HESITANT; TISSUE; STATUE; HAUNT; ASSENT

PAGE 149

Nobility

O	V	A	L		C	H	A	N	T		R	B	I	S
T	E	L	A		R	E	N	E	E		O	A	T	S
T	R	O	D		E	X	C	E	L		B	R	I	T
O	B	E	Y	E	D			E	M	B	O	S	S	
			G	R	I	M		S	T	E	I	N		
A	N	D	A	N	T	E		T	H	E	E	D	G	E
G	O	U	G	E		T	A	R	O	T		A	R	S
A	N	K	A		S	H	E	E	N		E	V	A	S
I	C	E		A	M	O	R	E		H	A	I	F	A
N	E	S	T	L	E	D		T	H	I	R	S	T	Y
		N	A	I	L	S		S	E	L	L			
D	R	I	V	E	L			R	O	C	K	E	T	
R	O	D	E		I	N	T	R	O		O	L	L	A
A	V	E	R		N	O	R	S	E		L	A	M	P
T	E	R	N		G	R	I	T	S		E	N	O	S

PAGE 150

Sport Maze

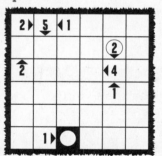

DOUBLETALK

SUITE/SWEET

PAGE 151

Word Sudoku

S	O	B	R	F	M	T	E	A
M	T	F	E	B	A	S	R	O
R	A	E	T	S	O	M	B	F
O	B	M	A	R	T	F	S	E
A	S	T	F	M	E	R	O	B
F	E	R	S	O	B	A	T	M
T	M	A	B	E	S	O	F	R
B	F	O	M	T	R	E	A	S
E	R	S	O	A	F	B	M	T

REPOSITION PREPOSITION

IN FACE OF

PAGE 152

Spot the Differences

WORD SHRINKS

STOOP ➡ STOP ➡ TOP ➡ TO

PAGE 153

Themeless

M	A	W	R		S	C	A	M	P		I	C	A	N
A	G	R	O		A	L	A	M	O		R	O	N	A
S	H	E	A		L	U	G	E	R		O	M	N	I
H	A	N	D	S	O	M	E		P	E	N	P	A	L
			S	H	O	P		T	O	S	I	R		
A	C	T	I	O	N		R	A	I	N	C	O	A	T
N	A	R	D	O		G	O	R	S	E		M	A	E
I	R	A	E		W	R	O	T	E		F	I	R	E
T	O	N		C	H	E	S	S		A	R	S	O	N
A	B	S	T	R	A	C	T		A	L	I	E	N	S
		P	H	O	T	O		F	R	A	T			
C	H	O	I	C	E		E	I	N	S	T	E	I	N
H	E	R	R		V	E	R	N	E		E	R	B	E
O	R	T	S		E	R	I	E	S		R	O	A	N
P	E	S	T		R	A	N	D	S		S	O	R	E

PAGE 154

BrainSnack®—Stained Glass

Window A. On all the other stained-glass windows, identically-colored pieces change in identical places.

BLOCK ANAGRAM

LACROSSE

PAGE 155

Collect

A collector actively looks for items; someone who saves items only ensures that nothing gets thrown away.

SANDWICH

STONE

PAGE 156

MLB Mascots

A	T	O	N		C	O	D	E	D		S	N	O	B
R	E	D	O		A	B	O	V	E		C	A	T	E
A	L	I	T		T	E	N	E	T		A	T	I	T
B	L	U	E	J	A	Y	S		R	E	L	I	S	H
S	Y	M	B	O	L	S		H	A	R	P	O		
			O	N	O		M	I	C	A		N	B	A
R	I	C	O		G	I	A	N	T	S		A	O	L
S	N	A	K	E		R	U	G		E	L	L	I	E
V	C	R		S	P	A	D	E	S		I	S	L	E
P	H	D		T	E	T	E		T	D	S			
		I	S	E	R	E		R	E	D	T	A	P	E
D	A	N	I	S	H		W	H	I	T	E	S	O	X
E	G	A	N		A	M	A	I	N		N	I	L	E
L	U	L	U		P	A	I	N	E		E	D	E	R
L	A	S	S		S	A	L	E	M		R	E	S	T

PAGE 157

BrainSnack®—Pick a Side

Angle 5. We see the back of the castle. The small tower on the left in front should be on the left in the back. The small tower on the right in back should be on the right in the front.

CHANGELINGS

BLACKSMITH
UNDERTAKER
LUMBERJACK

PAGE 158

Hip Hop

Hip hop lyrics often discuss things that go wrong in our world or the life of the hip hop artist.

UNCANNY TURN

CERTAINLY NOT

PAGE 159

Capital Namesakes

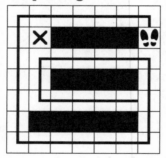

PAGE 160

Sudoku Twin

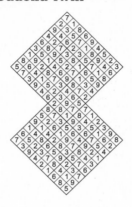

DOODLE PUZZLE

UNDERdog

PAGE 161

Keep Going

REPOSITION PREPOSITION

PREPARATORY TO

PAGE 162

Weather-Wise

PAGE 163

Monkey Business

The Outsiders
Talking in Whispers
Pink Lemon
Egg Drop
Shark in the Park
The Water Hole

DOUBLETALK

WOOD/WOULD

PAGE 164

Cats

If a cat does not have contact with humans during the first 60 days of its life then it cannot be socialized.

ONE LETTER LESS OR MORE

LIFEGUARD

PAGE 165

The Play's the Thing

L	O	G	O		A	G	A	M	A		P	H	I	L
E	C	R	U		R	A	Y	O	N		S	E	L	A
T	H	E	T	E	M	P	E	S	T		E	N	I	D
T	R	E	L	L	I	S		S	E	C	U	R	E	D
S	E	N	I	L	E				L	A	D	Y		
			N	I	S	I		D	O	N	O	V	A	N
F	A	C	E	S		D	R	I	P	S		I	P	O
L	A	Y	S		E	L	I	T	E		P	I	E	D
A	R	M		O	L	E	O	S		V	O	I	D	S
W	E	B	S	T	E	R		Y	E	A	R			
	E	P	I	C				S	P	R	I	N	G	
C	A	L	I	S	T	A		S	T	O	I	C	A	L
O	V	I	D		R	I	C	H	A	R	D	I	I	I
P	I	N	E		I	D	I	O	T		G	E	L	D
E	V	E	R		C	A	S	T	E		E	R	S	E

PAGE 166

Sunny Weather

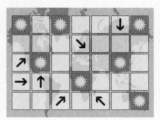

UNCANNY TURN

SCUM OF THE EARTH

PAGE 167

Concentration—Letter Division

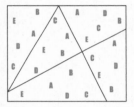

END GAME

B O O K E N D
E N D N O T E
L E G E N D S
T E N D I N G

PAGE 168

Big Words II

PAGE 169

The Puzzled Librarian

1) *Celebrity in Death*
2) *The Decameron*
3) *The Metamorphosis*
4) *A Perfect Blood*
5) *In the Night Kitchen*
6) *Defending Jacob*
7) *Lethal Marriage*
8) *The Naked and the Dead*
9) *Birdsong*
10) *Dune*

SANDWICH

BLACK

PAGE 170

Guitarists

The flamboyant American Jimi Hendrix is generally considered one of the best guitarists ever.

WORD SHRINKS

FORUM ➡ FORM ➡ FOR ➡ OR

PAGE 171

Futoshiki

1	4	5	3	2
3 > 2	4 < 5	1
5	3	2	1	4
4	1 < 3 > 2	5
2	5	1	4 > 3

LETTER LINE

SUBSTITUTE: SUITES; SUBSET; TUBES; TUTUS; BUST

PAGE 172

Word Pyramid

(1) a.m.,(2) arm, (3) mars, (4) smart, (5) master, (6) maestro, (7) upstream

ONE LETTER LESS OR MORE

ENLARGING

PAGE 173

BrainSnack®—Red or Green

Square I should be red. The green square on the second canvas determines where the red squares depart as infinite axes.

BLOCK ANAGRAM

FIGURE SKATING

PAGE 174

Big Words III

A	M	O	S		J	A	C	O	B		A	F	R	O
C	A	M	E		O	T	E	R	O		B	L	O	W
D	A	N	G	W	A	L	L	E	T		S	A	U	L
C	R	I	M	I	N	A	L		A	D	O	P	T	S
		E	R	N	S		S	N	E	R	D		
I	R	E	N	E	E		R	A	I	N	B	O	W	S
C	E	R	T	S		S	E	U	S	S		O	I	L
H	U	G	S		A	T	I	L	T		E	D	D	A
O	N	O		S	C	E	N	T		G	A	L	E	N
R	E	P	L	A	C	E	S		R	E	S	E	N	T
	H	U	M	I	D		L	E	N	T		
P	A	I	N	E	D		S	O	M	E	W	H	A	T
O	L	L	A		E	S	C	R	I	T	O	I	R	E
P	I	E	T		N	E	A	R	S		O	D	I	E
E	A	S	E		T	A	M	E	S		D	E	A	N

ANSWERS TO QUICK
AND DO YOU KNOW

p 15:   Mir space station
p 17:   Drew Barrymore
p 19:   Bon Jovi
p 21:   Lima
p 23:   Kyoto, Japan
p 25:   Cast
p 27:   Steven Spielberg
p 29:   Heart attack
p 31:   McDonald's
p 33:   Mia Farrow
p 35:   *Sex and the City*
p 37:   Talc
p 39:   Nelson
p 41:   C
p 43:   Eva Perón in *Evita*
p 45:   Burkina Faso
p 47:   Frank Gehry
p 49:   Janet Leigh
p 51:   *Titanic*
p 53:   Henry McCarty
p 55:   40 minutes
p 57:   500 sheets of paper
p 59:   South America
p 61:   Kate Moss
p 63:   *Apollo 13*
p 65:   Tallahassee
p 67:   *Aladdin*
p 69:   10—Germany, Austria, Slovakia, Hungary, Croatia, Serbia, Bulgaria, Moldova, Ukraine and Romania
p 71:   Jellyfish
p 73:   Theo
p 75:   Caribou
p 77:   Yugoslavia
p 79:   The *Titanic* (a Pekinese dog)
p 81:   George Clooney
p 83:   F. Scott Fitzgerald
p 85:   Serena
p 87:   George
p 89:   St. Petersburg, Russia

p 91:   J.M. Barrie
p 93:   Ginger
p 95:   Federal
p 97:   Tony Curtis
p 99:   Andy Gibb
p 101: Ken
p 103: Bit
p 105: Pizza
p 107: Lincoln
p 109: Dance
p 111: Pittsburgh
p 113: Paris
p 115: Tiger
p 117: Charles "Pete" Conrad
p 119: Eucalyptus
p 121: Tom Hanks
p 123: Egypt
p 125: Mercury
p 127: Shin bone
p 129: Arthur Hailey
p 131: One billion
p 133: A, B, AB and O
p 135: Plum tree
p 137: Victoria
p 139: An auction room
p 141: Angles
p 143: Benny Goodman
p 145: Trans-Canada
p 147: James Baldwin
p 149: Dead Sea
p 151: Italy
p 153: 26
p 155: "Love Me Do"
p 157: Sydney, Australia
p 159: Vitamin C
p 161: Ringing or buzzing in the ears
p 163: Howard Hughes
p 165: Ahab
p 167: Glenn Miller
p 169: Lewis Carroll
p 171: The *Jolly Roger*
p 173: Kukri